Histor

Financial History: From Barter to "Bitcoin" - An Overview of Our: Economic History, Monetary System, & Currency Crisis

Table of Contents

Introduction

Money makes the world go 'round, or at least that's what the famous song by R. Kelly as sung in the movie "Cabaret" says. Of course, this isn't literally true, but figuratively speaking, money is definitely what keeps the world ticking. There may be a few cultures in the world left where money has not yet replaced bartering, but as a whole, you can't get by without it.

And yet, money is something that is so commonplace that people rarely think about it anymore. How about you? When was the last time you really looked at the money you have in your hands and actually thought about how it came to be? Probably less than a couple of times throughout your life. It is such a shame that not many people are actually interested in learning more about money and finance in general because its history is so vibrant and full of interesting characters.

Take a moment to think about it. The paper that your money is printed on is in most cases worth far less than the amount printed on it. If you would try to sell a piece of paper that wasn't money for $20, people would laugh at you. And yet, when somebody sees the certified markings on a dollar bill, they don't hesitate. On the other hand, some coins actually have more value than the amount stamped on it, due to its metallic content. Copper pennies are actually worth more than one cent. And yet most people don't even think twice about using coins at face value. They know what it's worth, and they trust the system, even if they don't fully understand it.

In this book, you will learn more about how money came to be, and you will even get some information on its next stages of evolution. You will learn why people went from trading livestock to trading using real currency. You will learn why using money instead of directly trading is so important to a modern economy. You will also learn how the role that the Knights Templar played in the development of the modern banking system, and how the island of Yap used giant donut-shaped stones as a currency.

At the same time, we will also take a look at how money has shaped the world's history, and how you, as an individual can wisely invest your money. We will take a look at important economic terms, what the Federal Reserve Bank is all about, and what the gold standard is all about. We will also take an interesting look at debt, and how you, as a consumer, can choose to use debt wisely in order to increase your income and investments. We'll keep it interesting along the way with lots of little facts and interesting tidbits, and also take a look at what the future may hold for money.

These are just some of the things that you will learn from this book. I hope that by the end of the last chapter, you will have renewed interest about your money. If you have a deeper understanding of money, then perhaps you will learn to value it even more.

Chapter 1 – Early History of Currencies: From Bartering to Money

Money, in its many forms, actually does not have much value by itself. The amount of metal in a quarter does not have the same intrinsic value; this is even truer in paper bank notes. The value of money comes from its value as a means of exchange and as a portable store of wealth. Money is essentially a tool that helps make trading for commodities a whole lot easier. The only reason why money has value is that people agree that it is an acceptable mode of payment. It is, in essence, a middleman. This little coin or little piece of paper is purchasing power at your fingertips. It vouches for your ability to pay up.

However, there was a time when people did not have an organized means to measure the value of their goods, and during that time, trading was not just confusing, but also a whole lot more complicated. In this chapter we will take a look at the early origins of trading and money. How did civilizations get by without money? Are there still cultures in the world today that do not use money? How did people go from trusting a tangible object in front of them to trusting a little piece of paper? We will explore that and so much more, so hang on tight for the ride.

The Barter System

According to the Greek philosopher, Aristotle, in the early years in the history of humanity, there were no such things as coins or banknotes; in fact, there were no forms of currency at all. When people needed something from others, they will trade whatever goods they have for it. For instance, a hunter may trade the meat and furs of some of his kills in exchange for vegetables and grains. This is the Barter System. One problem with this kind of system is that there is no agreed upon measure of value; it often depends on the current needs of the traders, i.e. if one person is in dire need of animal pelts, he will most likely be more willing to accept an unfair trade. Today you can still see measure of value at work in the classifieds. One man's trash is another man's treasure, and while one person wouldn't even dream of paying for a certain object, the next person just may be willing to give you even more than what you are asking.

This subjectivity of value is one reason that drove people to use other objects as a means of measuring a commodity's worth. Another reason is that when bartering, you may not have something that the person you want to trade with desires. Take this example. You keep horses, and they are your means of livelihood. To get things that you need, you trade them frequently. A friend of yours makes shoes, and you could really use a new pair. You go to see if you can make a trade (after all, a horse is much more valuable than a shoe, right?). When you suggest a trade - your horse for shoes for everyone in your household - your friends reply is simple. He doesn't need a horse. In fact, he doesn't seem to need anything that you are able to trade. What he really needs are some better tools for making clothes. So off you go, to see if someone else has these tools, and if they are willing to trade with you, so that you can then in turn trade the tools for the clothes you need. You may have to go through quite a few trades before you actually get what you want. Money cuts out this problem. Think of it as a voucher. Instead of giving your friend a horse, you are essentially giving him a "voucher" to buy whatever it is that he needs. This saves you a whole lot of steps, and makes everyone happy at the same time.

Today, money has become the main form of exchange. However, in some remote parts of the world, there are ancient tribes that still use the barter system as their main means of exchange. Time periods of great poverty in history such as the Great Depression also encouraged bartering.

Outside of that there are even some opportunities for bartering in modern civilization. Just check out your local craigslist. In fact, there is even a TV show that airs on the History Channel called "Down East Dickering," that explores a bartering way of life for some people in Maine. Some culture still honor their history of bartering. In India, for example, a fair called Jonbeel Mela takes place every year at which the barter system is in full swing. People trade spices, vegetables, clothes, and other goods directly with each other, without the use of money. There are also quite a few online communities that are set up specifically for swapping certain items, such as books or clothing. Even more than bartering, these sites encourage simple trades, and leave the perceived price of items up to the individuals trading them.

The Gift Economy

The gift economy is a fairly simple idea. Instead of trading, you "gift" someone an item. However, in this kind of a society such a gift was given knowing that the person you gifted it to would be honorable enough to "gift" something back that was of equal or greater importance. In reality, it is the social pressure and expectations that would have made this type of a system work, and this type of economy would only work in a tight-knit community. All things considered, this system is not a true gift economy, as there are expectations for a return, and punishment if you do not return something of the correct value.

For many years, this theory of Aristotle has gone unchallenged, but recently, economist David Kinley had reason to believe that the Greek philosopher's theory was flawed. Kinley believed that Aristotle did not have sufficient understanding of how primitive communities lived, and that he may have formed his theories about bartering through his own conjectures and quite possibly from personal experience. Nevertheless, a French anthropologist, Marcel Mauss, believed to have evidence for the actual existence of such a society. The Kula tribe in the Trobriand islands were his prime example. However, it became hotly debated whether their system was only for the giving of gifts between individuals, or whether it was a means of exchange between two different factions or cultures.

David Graeber, an anthropologist, discovered that "gift economies" were actually quite common during the early days of humanity, or at least during the onset of the first agrarian societies. Graeber believed that early humans used an elaborate system of borrowing. Gift economies were most likely the first manifestation of the idea of debt in a society. Once you gave a gift, the other person was indebted to give something in return. Whether or not the refusal of the original gift was acceptable, is hard to tell. If it was not, then this type of system almost practices a type of forced debt. Graeber's research uncovered that money started to emerge when farmers started quantifying the amount of goods that they borrow/lend, for instance "I owe you one unit of grain". According to Graeber's research, people actually started dealing in credit before the first form of currency started to appear.

The Early Forms of Currency

Cattle – It may surprise many people to know that the oldest form of currency, at least the oldest known one, was cattle and other forms of livestock. Ancient Roman records showed that fines during the time were paid using cattle and other farm animals like sheep, goats, and oxen. You can even see instances of using cattle as a means of payment within the Iliad. Dowries were also very commonly paid by the means of livestock, and this even happens in some communities still today. In South Sudan, for example, cattle are still the sole acceptable means of payment of a dowry in some societies.

Cowrie Shells – Of course, people started to notice that it was quite inconvenient to lug around a cow or two whenever they need to buy things for their families, which is why they started using cowrie shells. Cowrie shells come from mollusks that live in the shallow waters of the Pacific and Indian Oceans. The Chinese were the first people to use cowrie shells as a means of currency. Cowrie shells are perhaps the one form of currency in history; in fact, some parts of Africa were still using cowries as late as the middle of the current century. Obviously this type of economy was limited more to coastal regions, as inland cultures did not have access to these types of shells.

Primitive Metal Currencies – In Ancient China, bronze and copper imitations of cowrie shells started appearing when they started noticing that cowrie shells were not that durable. These small metal imitations may well be the first form of coinage in the world. Around that same time, the Chinese still used weapons and tools as a means of trade, and then afterwards used miniature bronze replicas of the items; they actually used tiny daggers and arrows as a form of currency. After a while, the people got tired of accidentally stabbing their hands with tiny swords and spears that they changed the shape into much easier to handle circular pieces.

Early Stamped Metal Coins – Outside of China, the very first coins were made from small lumps of silver and gold stamped with the images of various gods and emperors as a proof of their authenticity. It was in the ancient city of Lydia, which is now part of Turkey, where archaeologists found the earliest use of stamped coins. Unlike the Chinese coins that used base metals like bronze and copper, the Lydians actually used precious metals like silver and gold.

Collecting ancient coins has become quite a pastime. It is a rewarding hobby, as there are countless different shapes and sizes of ancient metal coins. Unlike our modern coins, each individual coin is also unique. All coins were originally hand-cast, and the emblems, portraits, and artwork on them changed frequently. They can also be found in all sorts of different metals, including, but not limited to, gold, silver, copper, and bronze. Our modern coins are much more uniform. The U.S. penny is copper coated zinc, and the rest of the change is nickel. The Euro coins are also no longer made of precious metals. Even though the 20 and 50 cent pieces are made of "nordic gold," this gold is actually an alloy that is made up for the most part of copper with some aluminum, zinc, and tin mixed in. The other Euro coin pieces are nickel.

Leather Money – Besides coins, the ancient Chinese also made use of leather money. These one-foot square pieces of white deer hide decorated with colorful cloth borders. Despite being made of animal hide, these square pieces of leather are technically the first banknotes. However, this lasted for only a very short amount of time and was meant only to supplement the coinage of the country, as it was experiencing a shortage. The time period these banknotes were used was no more than 30 years. Still, the few remaining today are some of the most artistic and beautiful bills out there. In fact, it is quite surprising that more instances of leather money haven't been found. Leather is much more durable than paper, and can be manipulated just as easily.

Paper Money – the Chinese started using paper money at around 800 AD and its use continued until the early 15th century. The great thing about paper money is that it is easier to carry them around compared to heavy coins. Unfortunately, paper money was also quite easy to produce, and by the 15th century, so much paper currencies were in circulation that the resulting inflation almost made them worthless, and this caused the use of paper currency in China to disappear for a couple of centuries.

Paper money came about as a type of promissory note - a piece of paper issued by a bank and accepted as legal tender, that represented wealth in coins that you owned and was held by the bank. Its ease of production makes it incredibly simple to counterfeit, which has been the number one problem with paper money for centuries. In fact, the United States Secret Service was founded for the precise reason of tring to subdue counterfeiting operations. In 2006, roughly 65 million dollars were successfully passed off as real money that were actually counterfeit (that we know of), and an additional roughly 50 million dollars were successfully pulled out of circulation because the bills were detected properly. Outside the U.S., the $100 bill is the most counterfeited, whereas inside the U.S. it is the $20 bill. Following are a few measures that are taken to guard against counterfeit money in the United States.

Specific Paper Qualities

Did you know that American paper bills are actually not made from paper? They are rather a blend of cotton and linen, making the term cloth bills perfectly acceptable to describe them. The blend is hard to replicate and also has a specific feel to it. If you were handed a regular piece of paper that looked like a dollar bill, but felt like a piece of paper, chances are that you would immediately know that it was counterfeit. However, there are some types of paper that come very close to the feel of money. But there's a simple way to detect these. Have you ever noticed the bank using a pen on your bills when you made a deposit? This is called a counterfeit detector pen, and it works very simply. Because the money is made mostly out of cotton and contains no starch, the iodine in the pen does not react with it. However, if the paper is fake and contains other materials, the ink from the pen will turn color when marking the bill. Some counterfeiters try getting around this by taking actual $1 bills, bleaching them, and then printing them as $10 bills or higher in order to retain the correct substrate.

Watermark

This is a common countermeasure to counterfeit money. If you hold your money up to the light you will be able to see a watermark if the money is real. Creating a watermark is really fairly simple. Originally, bills were pressed with a metal plate dipped in water that contained an imprint of the watermark design. When pressing the metal onto the paper, the fibers at the place of the watermark become thinner, meaning that more light will shine through when you hold it up against the light. It really is a very simply technique, but hard to get right. With advances in pressing technique watermarks can now easily have a grayscale that makes them more complicated to replicate. Some bills have multiple watermarks, and some have an intricate design, while others merely echo the artwork that is printed on the bill. If you get passed a bill and there are no watermarks on it at all, you may be in trouble.

Microprinting and Raised Ink

While microprinting and raised ink are visible to the naked eye, they do take sophisticated equipment to replicate. Details such as these make sure that counterfeiting is hard, and expensive. It would take hours of fine tuning and a large investment in printing equipment to be able to replicate money efficiently and successfully.

Plastic Security Strip

Another feature in dollar bills worth $5 and up is a plastic security strip. This strip can easily be seen when held up to the light. These security strips were introduced in the 1990s and have been evolving ever since. Currently, the security strip is in a different location for each denomination, and it also glows a different color for each denomination when placed under an ultraviolet light. Conspiracy theorists have speculated that the security strip also contains RFID chips to help track the money, however, no evidence to back this up has been found. The simple rule of thumb is that you shouldn't trust a bill without it, unless it is, of course, a $1.00 bill.

Anti-counterfeiting options are constantly being researched. As the average lifespan of a dollar bill is only 5 years, it is easy to update the currency with safety features regularly. However, counterfeiters are still at work, regardless of how much security goes into it. That is one of the drawbacks of any kind of money.

No you have a basic idea about the development of currency in the world. These are but just a couple of the phases in the evolution of currency. However, you might have noticed that people early on valued convenience over security, seeing as most of the currencies presented did not have any safeguard against counterfeiting, and in the case of the Chinese paper currency, they also did not take into consideration the effects of inflation. However, as time passed, people gained a deeper understanding of finance, and this they developed until they came up with the beginnings of the banking institutions.

Throughout the years there have also been some very unique ideas when it comes to economies. Most of these are shaped by the culture surrounding them. A culture living in the jungle, for example, will find different commodities and items valuable than a culture living in a cold mountain climate. Because of this, the differences in economy in early human history are quite vast. Let's take a look at a few of these.

Spices

Numerous spices have been used as currency by different cultures and at different times, but probably the most common of these is salt. Throughout history, salt has always been an important commodity. Before the dawn of the industrial revolution and widespread refrigeration, salt was the number one preservative. People used it to put up meat and vegetables for the winter. The most prominent civilization to use salt as legal tender was Rome. We owe several modern expressions to this use, such as someone "being worth his salt," or the root of our word "salary," which literally means "salt money" from the Latin "salarium." The use of salt was also not restricted to only modern-day Europe. Marco Polo also described its use in Asia. As such, salt is one of the few commodities (next to gold) that has received world-wide recognition and worth.

Rai Stones

This type of currency is specific to the island of Yap in Micronesia. Literally, "rai" means "stone," and evidence suggests that stone has been used on Yap for millennia as a form of money. The irony about rai stones is that they are made of limestone, which is not found on the island of Yap. Rather, it was mined by the Yapese on the neighboring island of Palau. Even more interesting is that the Yapese traded beads, coconuts, and other goods for the right to mine the limestone on the island - in essence, trading one currency to receive another. In a sense this made their interaction one of the earliest forms of currency trading, which we will talk about more later.

Rai stones come in all sizes (up to 12 feet in diameter), and are flat, circular discs with a hole in the middle, so in a way they resemble a donut. The reason for the hole was to make transportation easier by sticking a pole through the stone. Still, the largest stones must have been very difficult to transport from one island to another due to their weight. Once on the island, the stones were also often set up in one location, and the owners never actually took possession. The stone stayed in its place, but ownership was constantly being bought and sold. In a way this was almost like owning a house in that it was an immovable object. Owning one of these stones was a great honor. Today, the U.S. Dollar is being used as currency in Yap, but rai stones are still an acceptable form of payment, especially for cultural or religious ceremonies.

Kissi Pennies

Kissi pennies are made out of iron, so in a sense they are not far off from the coins that are used in modern Western civilizations today. However, these are not your normal circular shaped coins. Instead, they are flat, finger-wide pieces of iron that are about a foot long, with two differently shaped heads - one resembles a foot, and one an ear. These pieces of metal are then often bundled together to make it easier to trade with. One bundle generally consists of 20 kissi pennies.

This type of currency was started in Sierra Leone in Africa, and spread to several of the surrounding countries. It is still in use in the area today, though using it has become a lot harder due to inflation. One bundle of kissi pennies used to be able to buy you quite a bit of food, whereas now you would require 4 or 5 bundles to get the same value. It is also no longer the main currency of the area, and is mostly used for cultural practices and rites such as the payment of a dowry.

Potato Mashers

This may be the oddest one yet. I mean, potato mashers? What a weird and odd object to use as currency! However, this truly used to be a currency in Cameroon, originating in a town called Bafia. In their society, potato mashers were extremely rare and only held by the more affluent in the community. Because of this, they became a prized possession to everyone in the area, and trading for a potato masher was always a good move, both for your wealth and your status in society. Potato mashers were almost a kind of status symbol, much like an expensive sports car would be in a modern culture.

Animal Pelts

The use of animal pelts for payment is a longstanding practice among humanity. In what used to be called New Netherland in the 17th century, beaver pelts were high in demand. The West India Trading Company shipped thousands of them back to Europe every year, making trapping a major player in early New England's economy. Trappers were able to use these pelts almost like they would money, as they held intrinsic worth to the society. Animal fur and leather were used in dozens of products, from shoes, to clothes, to saddles, holsters, hats, and briefcases. Most of these uses are still maintained today, and we have continued to integrate leather into new technology such as smart phones and vehicles.

New England wasn't the only place where pelts were of great value. In medieval times, squirrel pelts were used in Russia and Scandinavia as a form of payment. Thinking of how prolific these animals are, it makes sense that such a readily available and renewable resource would be used. Leather was in high demand, especially in the cold winters that are present in Scandinavia and parts of Russia. In a way the leather money used by the Chinese could also fall under this category, but usually it is regarded as closer to paper money than to fur-trading.

Bones

Bones have been used in ancient cultures as a type of currency, as well. The use of whale and dolphin teeth are the prime examples that have been found in ancient island cultures. Dolphin teeth have long been a form of currency on the Solomon Islands, until they were replaced with modern legal tender. Even then, however, dolphin teeth have remained a vital part of the culture, and there is a movement even today to return to the old form of trade. Of course modern animal rights activists would not be happy with the return of such a system, and there has been quite a bit of backlash and fighting going on over the idea.

Whale teeth are most known for their value in Fiji, where they are called tabua. Sperm whale teeth, specifically, held a very important place in Fijian society, and were not only used to trade as currency, but also represented cultural values. The owners of tabua were highly regarded. Today, tabua are still traded on the island, but they are mainly gifted as part of important cultural ceremonies. The hunting of sperm whale today is outlawed, so the tabua that are present are even more valuable, since more of them can't be added into circulation.

Quasi Universal Intergalactic Denomination (QUID)

Rather than an old currency, the quid is a currency that is not yet (or maybe never will be) in use, but holds an interesting idea for the future. It was created as a marketing gimmick to represent a future space traveling currency. While the idea seems ridiculous at present, it may actually yet prove to be of worth in the future. With more and more private companies tackling space exploration, this century may see a lot of new changes, including some in currency. The proposed "quid" are circular see-through discs with colored circles in the center, representing the planets in our solar system. They range in value from one to ten.

It is interesting to note that some of the items listed above are still a major part of our economy, but rather than taking the place of currency, they are now commodities that are traded on the stock market. Food and materials that are cornerstones of civilization will always retain an important place for a culture's wealth and economy, no matter what the currency is. But how did we move away from these more primitive forms of trade to a more regimented banking of currencies? In the next chapter, you will learn all about how the first banks came to be, and why they were so important.

But before we do that, let's take a look at some interesting currency facts from today. There are over 100 different currencies available in the world, and with that of course you have your most valuable and your least valuable. In the following we will determine the five strongest currencies, and the five weakest currencies.

Five Strongest Currencies

In fifth place is the Euro, which is at this time just slightly more valuable than the United States Dollar. It may surprise you that the U.S. Dollar is not in the top five, but it never has been. Since the introduction of the Euro in 1999, the Euro and the Dollar have been vying for the top position between the two. Currently, the Euro is winning, as it takes around $1.09 to buy one Euro. That being said, the relationship seems to be fairly stable, and has consistently been bouncing around the 1:1 ratio.

In fourth place is the British Pound. Considering that this currency is the oldest in the world with more than 1200 years of history, coming in 4th place really isn't bad. When the E.U. switched to the Euro, Britain decided to keep its currency. After all, switching to the Euro would mean that they were drastically devaluing their currency. Currently it takes about $1.40 to buy one British Pound. Britain takes great pride in its currency and the strength of its economy. Being an island, they were forced to conduct a lot of trading early on, which prepared them better than other nations for the global trading network that is present today.

Coming in in third place is the Omani Rial. Oman is a country that is located on the Arabian peninsula, but it didn't really make any headlines until after the 17th century. It holds an important trade position for both the Persian Gulf and the Indian Ocean, and is now also one of the top oil producers in the region. Oil earns its name as "black gold," which manifests itself in the fact that the top three currencies in the world all reside in oil country. It takes $2.60 to buy one Rial. Oman has continued to thrive and its currency shows no sign of weakening. Unlike other Arab countries, Oman has been able to diversify its production of commodities, mainly due to its strategic position on the map. This makes the country one of the most sought after stable sources of income from investments.

The second strongest currency in the world is the Bahraini Dinar. Bahrain is an island country that is comprised of several islands in the Persian Gulf. Though it is small, it has always held its own in history. Historians believe that this is where the Phoenicians originated, a strong seafaring people who specialized in trade. While oil does have something to do with the strength of its currency, Bahrain has today moved past oil production as its main industry, and instead specializes in banking and tourism. It is also the location of a United States military base, which brings a lot of work to the area as well. The Bahraini Dinar holds its own, and requires $2.65 to buy one unit.

Finally, the strongest currency in the world is the Kuwaiti Dinar. This may be surprising, as what you have heard in the news about Kuwait probably did not make it seem like a place that would be thriving economically. It is positioned between Iraq and Saudi Arabia and has been the location of countless regional conflicts. However, Kuwait owns the 6th largest oil reserves in the world, and oil has certainly played a huge role in making this currency as influential as it is, and probably also in the amount on conflict present in the area. Due to its thriving economy, Kuwait has become a hotspot for immigration. 70% of the nation's population is made up of expatriates, and only 30% are actually Kuwaiti people. It takes $3.30 to buy one Kuwaiti Dinar.

Five Weakest Currencies

Now that you know what the five strongest currencies in the world are, let's take a look at the five weakest currencies. The fifth weakest currency in the world is the Indonesian Rupiah. It takes nearly 10,000 Rupiah to purchase one U.S. Dollar. Indonesia is located in Asia and consists of a number of islands. Even though Indonesia is not a very large country, it has the 4th highest population of all countries in the world, and also ranks in the largest economies in the world. This makes it somewhat surprising that its Rupiah shows up on the list of weakest currencies. However, it does have a long history of inflation, which is why this currency takes fifth place.

In 4th place is the Dobra from São Tomé and Príncipe. Currently it takes almost 19,000 Dobras to buy $1.00. This country is an island in the Gulf of Guinea. As a country whose entire economy is almost exclusively built on plantation agriculture, it is not surprising that its currency has not quite been able to keep up with other currencies around the world. Economic growth has also proved difficult for the country on multiple occasions, making situations more challenging economically. Lack of resources on the island coupled with civil unrest have posed a constant challenge to the country. Nevertheless, the island keeps producing crops and maintaining its government, regardless of its weak currency.

Coming in in 3rd place is the Vietnamese Dong. Considering its history, it is not surprising that the economy of Vietnam has had its struggles. The Vietnam war and all the struggles brought with it certainly took a toll on the country. The clash of ideologies between communism and capitalism has also made it difficult for the country to move forward. However, in recent years the economy in Vietnam has shown to be quite promising, and it is one of the fastest growing economies in the world today. Hopes are that the Dong will continue to strengthen, but for the time being it takes a little over 20,000 Dong to buy $1.00.

In second place is the Somali Shilling. Somalia has a rich history of prosperous trade, however, in recent years it has been torn apart by civil war. The politics of an area greatly influence the economy and the worth of its currency, and Somalia is no exception. The region is still not entirely stable, and this has contributed to the poor performance of the Somali Shilling. It currently takes 22,000 Somali Shillings to buy $1.00. Until the civil war is ended and a more stable political system is put in place, the Somali Shilling will remain highly unreliable.

In first place, so the poorest performing currency in the world, is the Iranian Rial. Iran, much like Somalia, has an incredibly rich heritage. It is home to one of the oldest civilizations in the world, and is sometimes also referred to as Persia. Despite all this, finding it at the top of the list is probably not surprising to you, given the country's recent history of war. War generally takes a strong toll on economies, as well as currencies. The self-proclaimed Islamic State in the area has also not helped matters. In fact, the Islamic State has started coining its own currency, making things in the region even more complicated. Currently it takes almost 25,000 Rials to purchase just $1.00.

Unique Currencies

Now that you have an idea of the vast difference in currency worth, let's also take a look at some of the most unique currencies found in the world today, and in the past. These are all currencies that have moved past the bartering stages, yet each of these is unique in its own way.

1. Notgeld

After World War I, Germany was utterly destroyed economically. The peace treaties required reparations to be paid, and the country was entirely demilitarized. Morale was low, and the German Mark was worthless. However, this did not stop the Germans from figuring out a way to improve their situation. They began to make emergency money, or what was called "Notgeld." As paper and printing presses were not readily available, Germans thought of an easy way to print this money - on wood. Each piece of notgeld was carved out of small pieces of wood that resembled paper money.

2. Green Stamp Money

Vietnam had an interesting take on money for a while. They used a bill that had multiple denominations on the same piece of paper. You simply tore off the one you needed to make a payment, and then kept the rest to use later. The denominations were often also specific to a certain product, so that one of them could only be used for clothing, one for food, and so forth. In reality, this type of bill almost feels like a little coupon booklet. The only advantage it seemed to have was that is saved money in production. You didn't need to print a different bill for each denomination, as they were all together on the same bill - at least until they were torn apart and used.

3. The 100 Million Billion Bill

Yes, you read that right. 100 Million Billion - what? Pengos! This currency belonged to the country of Hungary during World War II, and it actually put into a production a 100 million billion pengo banknote. This, once again, demonstrated how big of an impact war and conflict have in currency, and vice versa. The amount of inflation in the country at the time was outlandishly high and made printing this bill a necessity. Somehow I don't think that this one will ever be outdone.

4. Transnistria's Stamped Notes

Transnistria is a patch of land located in Moldova, however, the people living there would claim otherwise. They have declared their own independence, but only three countries in the world have recognized them as such. As part of their movement to become independent, Transnistrians would take old Soviet banknotes and place their own stamp on them, in effect declaring it their own currency. Obviously there are a whole bunch of reasons why this did not work well, but it was still an interesting idea. Other countries, such as some Caribbean islands, also did the same with coins, except they would stamp a hole through the center of a coin, and then use it as their own legal tender.

5. Airtime Money

In a sense, airtime money isn't money at all, but a few countries in Africa treat it as such. They take their airtime minutes from their phones or other devices and use it as payment for goods or services instead of money. Apparently minutes for your phone are in high demand. Just like in previous cultures high demand products such as cattle and salt were used as currency, airtime money is being used as currency today.

As you can see, currencies have a rich history and exist in all kinds of shapes and forms. From barter to currency, and from cows to paper bills, each culture and time period has left its mark on the history of money. Now that you have a better idea of how currency came to be, let's take a look at the one institution that has devoted itself to all dealings with this currency - the bank.

Chapter 2 - History of Banking

The evolution of money coincides with that of the modern banking system; in fact, one cannot grow without the other. This symbiotic relationship paved the way for the widespread use of currency, and in effect, the growth of the world's economies.

As the use of currency began gaining popularity, people started looking for ways to make it much easier to use. Gold, silver and other precious metals were downright heavy and hard to transport, not to mention it makes it easier for highwaymen to rob merchants, which is why people needed something that will provide them with both security and convenience.

The Story of the Goldsmith

To give you some idea on how the very first bank started, you need to learn about the not-so-fictional story of the goldsmith.

The story goes, in Medieval Europe, the use of precious metals, gold in particular, started becoming more mainstream. It got even more popular when goldsmiths started minting gold coins in standardized sizes and purity, which made it easier to transact since the people no longer needed to weigh the amount of gold they traded. Since a goldsmith had to deal in huge amounts of precious metals, it was only reasonable for him to construct a highly secure and impenetrable vault where he could store his wares.

Eventually, the people also wanted a place to keep their money secure, so they knocked on the goldsmith's door and asked him for use of their private vaults, for a small fee of course. The goldsmith issued his depositors with claim checks that bore how much money they have in the vault so they can claim it later if they wish. Eventually, the merchants started accepting claim checks as a viable means of currency, since they could withdraw the deposit themselves if they have a valid document.

As this practice of using claim checks got more mainstream, the people actually preferred to use them instead of the real precious metals that they have in the goldsmith's vault. This sudden interest in claim checks gave the goldsmith a good idea on how he can use the money to earn even more profit.

The times during Medieval Europe were hard, which is why many people would ask the goldsmith for loans to help tide them over until they got back on their feet. The goldsmith figured that his depositors would seldom withdraw their money from his vaults, and even rarely would two or more of them would withdraw at the same time; this meant there was a large hoard of money in the vault at any given time.

This gave the goldsmith an idea that he could lend out his depositors' money to other people and charge interest for the loans. This worked out great for the goldsmith because as long as the borrowers repaid their debts, the depositors can still withdraw their money whenever they want.

Thanks to this newfound system, the goldsmith actually became wealthier, which made the townspeople suspicious. They demanded the goldsmith to show them if their money was still in the goldsmith's vault, and since the goldsmith was careful enough not to lend out too much of his depositors' money, he still had a reasonable store to show them and appease their suspicions. However, the depositors demanded that they get a share of the profits that the goldsmith gets from giving out loans using their money, to which the latter agreed. The depositors received small interest payments while the goldsmith held onto the bigger chunk of profit, and this is how modern banking came about.

This is just an allegory of how the first banks came about, but this does provide enough facts that will help you understand how the need for security caused the banking system to exist, and why progress made it stay.

Early Evidence of Banking

Nevertheless, the idea of lending and saving money has been around almost as long as written history. In order for a society to exist, its members must have a way to trade and interact economically. If you don't want to be doing this directly and in person all the time, you need some sort of institution to be the middleman. Regardless of whether a lending note is typed into a digital screen or engraved onto a piece of stone, its purpose is the same. In this sense, banking has been around just as long as human civilization has been, but it has been ever evolving at the same pace of technology and currency in general.

Written record of banking interactions have been dated as far back as ancient Mesopotamia. An excellent example of this are the Murashu Tablets, which were excavated near the ancient city of Nippur, which resides South of modern-day Baghdad in Iraq. These tablets demonstrate the banking activities of "Murashu & Sons," a local banking family, or company, if you will. Its primary interactions were with Jewish people who had remained in Babylon after their exile, and date to the 5th century B.C. After the Jews were taken captive by the Babylonian empire, they were allowed to return to Israel after a certain amount of time. Not everyone, however, chose to return. This left a subculture in the Babylonian Empire. Murashu & Sons served this subculture. Economists have debated whether or not these tablets actually signify banking in the modern sense, and experts have fallen on both sides of the debate.

Shortly after this period there are also records available in Greece that demonstrate the existence of creditors in a form of banking. At this time, metal coins were also already in use instead of other pre-money forms of currency, making the idea of lending and borrowing much easier. Outside of such creditors or "banks," the main places for economic transactions in ancient times were either at palaces or in temples. As most early forms of government centered around a monarchy or dictatorship, it makes sense that the palace would be a place of commerce. The ancient temple, regardless of religion, was also a center for culture and community, making it a logical place for transactions, as well.

In countries like Egypt and Rome, baking has also been proven through written record. In India there are records dating as far back as the 18th century B.C. In short, the lending and borrowing transactions between people are well documented, as far back as documents are in existence.If you study the advance of technology in human history, you won't be able to avoid also studying the advances in banking.

The Emergence of Merchant Banks and the Knights Templar

Merchant banks began to emerge at the beginning of the middle ages, and, as the name suggests, were primarily intended for trade. Individuals rarely used banks at this time. Rather a merchant bank was a place that provided loans to companies in exchange for a share in that company. In a sense, merchant banks are also at the root of our modern stock exchange system. They began to emerge along the trade routes to Asia and the Middle East, especially in conjunction with the silk trade. The idea was transferred into other businesses, as well. It wasn't long until another historical event would take advantage of the idea of banking.

During the 12th century, the Crusades were still in full swing, and in order to finance such a huge undertaking, it sparked the need for the emergence of the first modern banking institution. The Crusades prompted King Henry II of England to collect taxes in support of the war in the Holy Land, and the money collected were stored in the coffers of the Knights

Templars, which were scattered in castles all over Europe. This led to the practice of merchants depositing their money in one of the Templars' castles, where they will receive a demand note that stated just how much money they deposited. This made traveling much easier for the merchants because they would not be carrying their money with them, which meant that robbers and highwaymen would not get a single coin from them.

When they reach their destination, they only need to travel to the nearest Templar-controlled castle, surrender their demand letter and they will get back the amount they deposited, minus a small operational fee of course. The impressive thing about this type of baking in comparison to past efforts, was that the bank actually spanned multiple countries. It wasn't like a local bank that only had one branch. This was an actual network of banks.

The oldest bank in the world that is still active today was founded just a short time after the crusades, in 1472 as the Mount of Piety, which is today the Banca Monte dei Paschi di Siena. This bank, which was founded in Sienna, Italy, is amazingly the third largest bank in Italy today, with dozens of branches around the country. Imagine the kind of innovation and change a company would have to go through to keep its doors open that long. Pretty incredible!

The Royal Abuse of Banking

As the strength of the banking institutions grew, they gained the attention of various European monarchs, and since they were able to operate with the blessings of the ruling monarchy, the banks offered the rulers special offers regarding loans; sometimes they would not even charge interest. This easy financing platform tempted kings into leading lavish lifestyles, and often this easy access to funds also meant that they can go into costly wars with their neighboring kingdoms and their coffers would not suffer that large of a hit. However, there were times when the ruling monarch took up too large of a debt than he could handle.

One such time was during the rule of King Phillip II of Spain. King Phillip somehow managed to rack up so much debt from banks because of his engaging in pointless wars that he actually caused the first recorded instance of national bankruptcy, and as if that wasn't enough, King Phillip II also caused the second, third, and fourth instances, all in rapid succession. The reason Spain went bankrupt was because its national debt was so high that more than 40% of its Gross National Product went to paying off the interest and some part of the main debt amount. Today, it is almost unheard of for a government to declare bankruptcy. In fact, it is constitutionally outlawed in the United States through an amendment. We will talk a little more about this later when we take a look at currency trading and debt.

The First Modern Bank

The very first bank to issue banknotes was the Bank of England, established in 1695. These banknotes were once hand-written and was issued to the person upon depositing money to the bank, or when taking up a loan. However, in 1745, the Bank of England started printing standardized banknotes of different denominations, but these notes still required the writing of the payee's name and the signature of the bank's cashier. Fully printed notes did not start appearing until more than a century after the establishment of the bank.

Before, the rules against usury, or the charging of interest against personal loans, prevented Jews and Christians from practicing the usual banking practices. These two religions had a strong influence on the government at the time, so the views regarding interest and usury of the church were generally adapted by the country as law. However, the rise of Protestantism freed many European Christians from the edicts of usury, which led to a sudden increase of the services offered by many banks. Today, religions rarely have an impact on financial policy of a country in the modern Westernized world. However, it is still very common in countries with a strong muslim population that the religious views on finance and money must be followed.

The Emergence of Central Banks

A central bank is basically the bank that other, smaller banks use. To be more specific, it is a bank sanctioned by the government with specific duties to support the performance of the country's economy. The central bank is in control of the money supply to prevent inflation and promote stability of the economy.

The very first central bank in the world is the Swedish Riksbank. However, the one that is more popular and recognizable is the Bank of England. The Bank came to be when England got into a bit of financial trouble during the Nine Years' War against France. The government needed to borrow around £1,200,000 (at 8% interest), but the credit of King William III was so horrible that no banker would even dream of lending the monarch the money.

To induce the banks to lend the government the money it needed, the loan subscribers were incorporated by the name of the Governor and the Company of the Bank of England. The government also granted the newly established Bank of England certain long-term privileges that other banks do not have, like the issuance of banknotes. Basically, the bank promised to help the government, if the government promised to help the bank. This marked the first emergence of a bank similar to what we have today in the Federal Reserve Bank, and is also one of the reasons why there is a movement to end the Fed. Some people believe that the government is unfairly favoring a particular company in order to receive benefits in return. However, this type of interaction has been so ingrained in culture through the last few decades of history, that getting rid of this relationship would be very difficult indeed.

Although many do consider the Bank of England as the first central bank in the world, it previously did not have the kind of power that modern banks had. For example, the Bank did not have the ability to regulate the value of the national currency, the ability to finance government projects and undertakings, and the power to bail out smaller banks that got into deep financial trouble. So in a sense, the government has been granting a central bank more and more power ever since it started down this path.

Continuing Evolution of Banking into Modern Day

Two notable names to remember in the development of modern banking are Henry Thornton and the Rothschild family. Henry Thornton lived in the late 18th century and is often described as the father of the modern central bank. He was one of the main members of a bank in London called Down, Thornton, and Free. This bank became one of the strongest banks of the time. His theory of banking and strong support for the emerging system as a minister of parliament are his greatest legacy. He was also an influential figure in the push to abolish slavery and make peace with the emerging American nation.

The Rothschild family are notable for several reasons, and have shaped banking from the 18th century on even until today. The first notable Rothschild member was Mayer Amschel Rothschild, a German Jew who was the beginning of what would be a family banking business to last for centuries. Their main legacy is the promoting of international banking. They were the first private banking family to have a large impact on the economies and politics of the world. Their banks specialized in the trade of gold bullion, which is why their bank in London was the location for the gold fixing for almost the entire 20th century. Some of the important international dealings they were involved with were the building of the Suez Canal, as well as financing the Japanese in their fight with Russia from 1904-1905. The French side of the family also helped fund French wars in the Napoleonic era.

By this time it was clear that banks were not just small private businesses. They could hold quite an influence on the world and the economy. To hold any amount of power in the modern world, a financial institution would need to be by your side and have your back. The connection between currency and politics, however, has always been present. This idea also becomes obvious when considering the fact that influential people are often pictured on currencies. Let's take a look at some notable people that have earned a face on one of the over 100 currencies present in the world today.

Mak Dizdar, Bosnian and Herzogovinian Convertible Mark

Mehmedalija, or Mak Dizdar, was born in what was then Austria-Hungary at the beginning of the 20th century. He is today one of the most influential poets in Bosnian and Herzogovinian history. His sister and mother were killed in a concentration camp in World War II, which strongly influenced his writings. His poems are mystical and blend Bosnian culture, Christianity, and Islam into a surreal picture of life and death.

Thérèse Casgrain, Canadian Dollar

Thérèse Casgrain is most known in Canada, and specifically Quebec, for her endeavors as a suffragette. She pushed hard for women's rights in politics. She came from a family of liberal politicians, and was herself a strong-willed and independent woman. Her greatest achievement was as the first female leader of a political party in Canada. She also had the honor to hold a seat in the Canadian Senate for 9 months at the ripe old age of 74.

Policarpa Salavarrieta, Colombian Peso

Otherwise known as La Pola, this famous lady from Colombia is best remembered for her fight for Colombian independence from Spain. She was a known revolutionary and spy who took work as a seamstress for Spanish Loyalists in order to overhear their conversations and report important news back to the revolutionaries. She was eventually captured and executed by firing squad at the young age of 22. Despite her short life, she left an indelible mark on Colombian history.

Ibn al-Haytham, Iraqi Dinar

After the fall of Saddam Hussein, whose image had been on all Iraqi currency, the country did not have to look far to find someone worthy of a position on their money. al-Haytham, or otherwise known as Alhazen, was an Arab scientist, mathematician, astronomer, and philosopher, who lived in the 11th century. Alhazen is most recognized as one of the first scientists to use validated scientific method, and for has work in optometry and astronomy. He is often called the second Ptolemy, which is fitting, as Alhazen scrutinized Ptolemies works with a fine-toothed comb and pointed out corrections that needed to be made.

Samuel Sharpe, Jamaican Dollar

Samuel, or Sam Sharpe, is the most notable figure in the Jamaican fight against slavery. He was behind the slave rebellion of 1832 that was known as the Jamaican Baptist War. The name of this movement is derived from the fact that Sharpe was a Baptist preacher. He was well-educated, and spent his free time educating other slaves on the island in Christianity. His hope and goal was to bring freedom to all the slaves. He was executed at the age of 31 for his efforts. It was only a few years following his death that slavery would indeed be abolished by the British Empire.

Ladi Kwali, Nigerian Naira

Ladi Kwali is remembered as an artist for the beautiful pots and pottery techniques she used. Pottery is an intrinsic part of female Nigerian culture. It is a means to both create useful items, but also enhance lives with beauty. Ladi Kwali became so recognized as a potter, that she later toured the world and had pottery exhibits as far as England. Nigeria recognizes her as one of their most outstanding artists in the 20th century.

Mimar Kemaleddin, Turkish Lira

As you can see, we have had various artists, revolutionaries, scientists, and political figures represented on bill so far. Mimar Kemaleddin, on the other hand, was an architect. He attended engineering school in Turkey, and then also furthered his studies in architecture for two years in Germany. He is most remembered not only for his beautiful buildings that combine a European and Middle Eastern influence, but also for his work as a teacher and a founder of Society of Ottoman Architects and Engineers.

Theodoros Kolokotronis, Greek Drachma

It makes sense that military leaders would also have their place on the currencies of the world. Theodoros Kolokotronis, a Greek general, played an important role in the war against the Ottoman Empire in the Greek War of Independence. He had numerous decisive victories against the enemy, and became a legend among the people of Greece. His place on their currency is well earned.

Paper currencies have certainly also expanded the artistic side of currency. The design options are endless compared to the designs available for coins. You have more space, and color is an option.

The Future of Banking

Of course, the greatest shift in banking in recent years has been influenced by technology. The internet and the connectivity of the world made things possible that in prior years would have never been possible. Private individual investors can easily use online tools to instantly become involved in financial institutions or hold stock in different companies. We are also seeing a strong shift from paper to the proverbial plastic. Fewer and fewer people pay with cash, or even check. Transactions can be made on our computers, our phones, and even our watches. Credit cards can be accepted by anyone with the help of small, cheap devices. Individuals are connected more than ever, and the stock markets are bigger than ever as well. It will be interesting to see where this continuing evolution of economy will take us in the future, especially since some entirely digital currencies are already in existence, which we will talk about more in depth in a later chapter.

In this chapter, you have learned about how banks operations were limited by the amount of precious metals they have in their coffers, otherwise known as the gold standard. However, this standard of banking is now seldom used by central banks of nations all over the world. We will look at how the banks moved away from the gold standard in more detail in a later chapter. But first, we will take a look at how the history of money has always been closely related to the history of war and conflict.

Chapter 3 - The Role of Money in the World's Major Conflicts

It is apparent that money and politics go hand in hand. Most governments have control over their currency in some way or another, and this has greatly shaped the world's history. In fact, money has played a vital role in just about every human conflict in history. After all, in order to fight a war you need money. Money to pay soldiers, to buy weapons, and to rebuild. Let's take a look at some of the major conflicts and discover how money and the economy has played a vital role in each of them.

The Mercenary War

As its name suggests, the Mercenary War is probably the most clear example of the impact of money on national conflict. It took place between 240 and 238 B.C., shortly after the first Punic War, which was a war that took place between Rome and Carthage. As was custom at that time, Carthage employed mercenaries to help fight the war for them. Hiring mercenaries was a sure way of getting the job done, as these men were highly motivated since you only got paid if you stayed alive. Carthage, however, did not fair very well, and was defeated by Rome. The city was left destitute, and was unable to pay its mercenaries due to damages that had to be paid to Rome.

The mercenaries, however, did not take kindly to this situation. They had risked life and limb and were determined to force Carthage to pay, at sword point if necessary. But they soon found out that Carthage truly was destitute. Even if they had won the war there was no money there to pay them with. Luckily for Carthage they were able to defeat the mercenaries and quell the movement before it got out of hand. When it all comes down to it, the Mercenary War was fought over money - plain and simple.

Filling King John's Coffers

This period in history, as well as much of the crusades, were marked by conflict that was not caused because of money. However, the conflicts that arose had a strong impact on the wealth of nations involved. King John in England was no exception. His plan was to reclaim Normandy, a portion of land in France that had been owned by England up until recently before John took the throne. In order to launch his campaign, however, he would need an exorbitant amount of money, and England's coffers were looking rather bare.

In order to raise the money that he needed, King John enacted a number of very unpopular taxes and levies. For example, King John levied scutage payments, even though it was not a time of war. Traditionally, scutage payments were a sum that could be paid to get ouf of military service if the country was at war. The fact that King John was brazen enough to collect these payments even during times of peace was an outrage to most citizens. He also enacted a new tax that was equivalent to the modern income tax. This had never been done before, either. It is no small wonder that King John is one of the most despised and unloved monarchs in British history. The modern-day Libertarian cry of "taxation is theft" was mostly likely on the lips of every English citizen at the time.

But not everything that came out of King John's reign and his greed for money was bad. The problems he created led to the creation of the Magna Carta, which held in it the keys to modern forms of government. Almost all the components of our bill of rights can be found in the magna carta. So at least something good came out of King John's reign.

The Napoleonic Wars

The Napoleonic Wars demonstrate how money has also been used as a weapon in conflict. Britain and France had been at war off and on for hundreds of years, even further back than the Battle of Hastings in 1066. When Napoleon took power, Britain became his biggest enemy. In 1806 he proclaimed the Continental System, which sought to isolate Britain from the continent by blocking it from all form of trade. By isolating Britain in this way, he thought he could crumble their economy and bring the country to its knees.

But Napoleon's plan did not work. As an island nation, Britain had built a very strong and self-sufficient industry and trading network with its colonies. It proved, if nothing else, that it could do just fine without trading with continental Europe. In fact, Britain was wealthy enough to subsidize soldiers from other countries to support its own military in the fight against Napoleon. Rathern than mercenaries, subsidizing soldiers simply meant that Britain helped pay for the outfitting of another country's military. Without the economic strength and wealth that Britain had built, Europe would have most likely fallen to Napoleon. The face of the modern world would be entirely different today if it weren't for how money was spent in the Napoleonic Wars.

The Boer Wars

This war is one that you may have never heard of before, but it is representative of the struggle between colonies and their colonizers. Just as in the American revolution, the inhabitants of South Africa felt that they were being unjustly taxed and ruled by the British. Money played a large role in the motivation for independence, and the monetary hit for Britain was a significant consequence of the war.

The First Boer War was won by South Africa in 1881 after a year of fighting. They declared their independence, and Britain was forced to retreat. However, the revolutionaries did not fare as well in the Second Boer War, and Britain regained control of the country in 1899. For the time being, Britain had averted a monetary disaster by winning back its colony. The Boer Wars were a sign of things to come, as countries with colonies would slowly lose them to independence over the next 150 years. This would create new economies and currencies, and force countries like Britain to strengthen their own economy through other means than colonization.

World War I and The Great Depression

World War I and the Great Depression had a huge influence on the economies of the world and on the way that we deal with money. The time of war brought an economic boost, which was then followed by the Great Depression, only to be followed by yet another war. The impact this all had on currency and wealth cannot be over exaggerated.

The biggest change this brought was the slow move away from the gold standard. It is interesting to note that the Great Depression occurred not long after the creation of the Federal Reserve in 1913. Some theories as to the cause of the Great Depression hold the Federal Reserve accountable. Others hold the inability to perform quantitative easing with a gold standard accountable. Regardless, the Great Depression impacted both the United States and the world. As we will discuss in the coming chapter, Britain was the first to move away from the gold standard, but the United States followed soon after.

In 1933, Franklin Delano Roosevelt signed an executive order that required all Americans to sell all of their gold coin, bullion, and bars back to the Federal Reserve, with the exception of a small allowed amount. His excuse was that people were hoarding gold because they were afraid from the Great Depression. At the time, the Federal Reserve was required to hold 40% gold backing for the currency that was in circulation. The bank had reached its limit, and was not able to print any more money, as it had no more gold. The executive order signed by FDR was a way for the Fed to get the gold it needed in order to print more money. Of course, many speculate that FDR already had in mind that he would abandon the gold standard. Ridding the individual citizen of gold would just make the transition easier.

Another impact World War I had on world economies and currency was requiring Germany to pay reparations after the war. The country was already completely demilitarized and demoralized, and paying of the reparations left it entirely destitute. This vacuum of power in the country led to a poor morale that paved the way for a ruler like Hitler to take power.

As you can see, conflict and money go hand in hand throughout history. Perhaps the saying that the love of money is the root of all evil has something to it. There are also many theories out there that submit the claim that almost every modern war fought in the last 50 years has been primarily motivated by money. Of course, multiple factors go into every conflict, but money certainly plays its part. In the next chapter we will take a closer look at the gold standard and what it means for us today.

Chapter 4 – The Rise and Fall of the Gold Standard

In the old days, countries were only allowed to circulate a certain amount of their currency based on the amount of gold that they have in their reserves. Put simply, the value of a country's money depends largely on the amount of gold said country has. The country would set a fixed price on an ounce of gold, and this would set the value of said currency.

For instance, if the United States were to declare that an ounce of gold would cost $20, it means that every dollar is worth 1/20th of an ounce of gold. In those days, when you go to the banks and exchange your banknotes for its gold equivalent, you will get a gold coin that coincides with the amount you exchanged.

This practice went on for centuries after the use of gold and silver became mainstream, but these days no country in the world uses the gold standard anymore.

History of the Gold Standard

Gold has always been an important part of history. In and of itself as a raw material, its uses are limited to the artistic, and some technological uses. You can't eat gold, and yet we as humans have always valued it. Of course, it is undeniable that it is beautiful, and it is also imperishable. Tombs decorated in gold have been found in Egypt that date to over 5,000 years ago. At the same time, gold has never been found in the same abundance as other resources such as coal or oil (sometimes called black gold). Perhaps this is what has made it so valuable from the beginning.

It is also interesting to note that gold has been important in every culture around the world. For whatever reason, people groups from the Incas in South America to the Aborigines in Australia, valued gold and gave it a place in society. Perhaps this is one of the reasons that gold evolved into an international standard of wealth, recognized by countries everywhere. In the history of the world it is estimated that around 174,000 tonnes have been excavated, which translates into around 21 square meters of gold. Gold is still being mined today at an increasing rate equivalent with the world's population, but it is being used less and less in economies.

Gold began to be used as money thousands of years ago. The first place that this practice became prevalent was Asia Minor. It is in this area that the oldest gold coin was found, a ⅙ stater that is 2,700 years old. It is made up of natural electrum, an alloy that consists of gold and silver. On it is a lion's head, and it is thought that it originated in a small town called Lydia. Herodotus even mentioned the presence of gold near Lydia in his histories. These early coins were measured by weight and were literally "worth their weight in gold."

During the periods that came to be known as the early and high Middle Ages, the currency used throughout the Mediterranean and Europe was the Byzantine gold solidus which was also called the bezant. As the Byzantine Empire collapsed, so did the bezant. Instead, many European principalities started using silver as the currency in the place of gold. This eventually led to the development of silver standards. Silver remained the standard currency for most nations for a long time, even up to the founding of the United States.

The first place to adopt a gold specie standard was the British West Indies in the early 18th century. This was the *de facto* gold standard that was based on the Spanish doubloon. The doubloon was a solid gold coin that weighed a little less than the ancient stater at about ¼ of a troy ounce, a measurement that has been used for metals for hundreds of years, and is heavier than a U.S. ounce. In 1717, Sir Isaac Newton, who was then serving as the master of the Royal Mint, put Britain on a gold standard and pretty much drove silver out of circulation by establishing a new mint ratio between gold and silver.

All in all, there are three different types of gold standards. The gold specie, the gold bullion, and the gold exchange. To have a gold specie standard, a gold coin must be in circulation, upon which the value of all other bills and coins are based. In the gold bullion standard, the circulating money is still fixed on a gold standard, however, there are no gold coins in circulation. It is possible to buy bullion at a price, but gold itself is not used as a means of currency. The gold exchange standard relates to the interaction between countries, in which a government guarantees a particular exchange rate with another country's currency, as long as that currency is based on a gold standard as well.

In 1821, a formal gold specie standard was instituted. Britain adopted this standard after the gold sovereign was introduced by the Royal Mint. Later on, other countries such as the United States of America, the United Province of Canada, Newfoundland and Germany also adopted gold. Germany started the gold mark, the United States started using the gold eagle and Canada used a dual system that utilized both the gold sovereign and the gold eagle.

Eventually, the gold specie standard ended in the United Kingdom and the British Empire when World War I broke out.

Why Did Countries Abandon the Gold Standard?

The abolition of the gold standard started, ironically, where the concept of central banking came from, the Bank of England. During the Great Depression in 1931, the English people started to fear that the world as they knew it was starting to collapse, so they started exchanging the paper money they had for real gold. This massive withdrawal of gold almost got to the point when the Bank of England almost ran out, which terrified Montagu Norman, the then head of the bank.

One day, Norman simply collapsed due to the immense pressure on his shoulders. The fate of the entire Western civilization was in his hands, and he could not think of a way to get out of this problem. He just could not bear the thought of leaving the gold standard because it was the only thing that was keeping the economy together.

He had to take an extended leave of absence because he could not function anymore as the head of the Bank of England. While Norman was gone, the colleagues he left behind had to swallow their pride and accept the fact that they have no other choice; they took the Bank of England off the gold standard.

This decision to leave the gold standard reverberated all over the world, people all over the world started trading in their money for gold before their own economies started leaving the standard, and it eventually found its way across the pond to the United States.

Franklin D. Roosevelt just experienced the mother of all bank runs during his term as the President of the United States, and he knew that the gold standard was the cause of the problem, but he did not know what he could, or should do about it. All but one of his economic advisors told Roosevelt to stick it out with the gold standard; they said that things would tide over eventually.

This one adviser that told him to ditch the gold standard, George Warren, whom his colleagues regarded as a "crank", was actually an agricultural economist, but he also did some in depth studies about the gold standard and how it was affecting the economy in a negative manner. Much to his other advisors' surprise, FDR listened to Warren and took the US off the gold standard.

Surprisingly, it was actually beneficial for the United States to get off the gold standard, almost all of the economists nowadays even said that this was the reason the country survived the Great Depression. However, it wasn't until 1970 that the United States completely cut the cord between gold and the dollar. This was the year that President Nixon canceled any direct international conversion between the dollar and gold across the board. Once the United States and Britain were off the gold standard, other countries slowly followed. Mainland Europe, Asia, and other areas of the world who held to gold saw that it was working for Britain and the U.S.A., and decided to follow suit. Not surprisingly, Switzerland was the last hold-out, and did not abandon the gold standard until the year 2000. Today, there are no countries left that hold to it.

What Are the Current Pros and Cons of Returning to a Gold Standard?

The gold standard has both proponents and detractors. Each side makes good and solid points for why a return to the gold standard would or would not be advisable. Here are a few of them.

Pros

Throughout history, gold has had a value that has been understood and accepted throughout the world. It was first minted as gold coins by the King of Lydia (which lies in modern day Turkey) in 550 BC. Paper money essentially has no real value. It is a form of currency because the government says so. In essence, it has value because of what is known as the 'full faith and credit' of the government. This is called fiat money. The problem with this is that if the people lose trust in it, its value will plummet. Just like there was a rush to buy gold in England, the same thing could happen in any other country, regardless of whether they are part of a gold standard or not. The pro with the gold standard is that a run on the banks could be survived if a gold standard is being kept up. If this type of scenario occurred without a gold standard in place, banks may be forced to shut their doors. There is also the fact that gold has intrinsic value due to its rarity, beauty and utility.

Another argument for gold is that it restricts the ability of the government to print money at will thus limiting the government's power. In a fiat currency the government doesn't have to base the manufacture of money on any tangibles and can do so whenever it wants to. When the United States left the gold standard in 1971, the U.S. currency in circulation was around $48.6 billion dollars. In 2012, this amount had increased to $12 trillion. If a gold standard were in effect, new money could only be printed if the country had the gold to back that currency. This would effectively check the growing power of the government.

Some argue that the current fiat monetary system prevalent in the United States is undemocratic. In case of a gold standard, market forces would determine the supply of money. However, currently the supply is in the hands of a central banking committee (the Federal Reserve), which can determine whether the supply of money is to be increased or reduced. Besides seeming to be undemocratic, it also appears anti-capitalist. In the same vein as already discussed, the government is too involved in money printing without the presence of a gold standard. Basically, the government gets to set the rules without the permission of the people for specific occasions.

There are those who believe that returning to a gold standard would also help reduce inflation rates and consumer price rises would also slow down. Fewer regulations have often been shown to encourage free enterprise and competition, which in turn brings the cost down for the consumer, while still leaving the company with a bigger profit margin. With a gold standard, everybody wins, except for government bureaucracy.

As per history, when the United States was on a gold standard, it had lower rates of inflation. This can be seen when comparing the periods between 1880 and 1913 and 1971 and 1979. The inflation in the former period (1880-1913) was around 1.6% per year; this was when the gold standard was in effect. In 1971, President Richard Nixon took the United States off the gold standard entirely. At this time, inflation was around 3.3%. In 1979, the inflation rate had hit 13.3%. This astronomical rise in inflation rates wasn't just prevalent in the United States. Studies conducted by Federal Reserve economists on 15 countries showed that when the country in question operated under a gold standard the annual inflation rate was 1.75% on an average. When the country was not operating under a gold standard, this average annual inflation rate skyrocketed to 9.17%. Moreover, between 1971 and 2003, 80% of the purchasing power of the dollar was lost due to inflation. In fact, in 2011 the purchasing power of one dollar was on par with the purchasing power of 19 cents in 1971.

Trade deficits could also be reduced by returning to the gold standard. In the fiat money system that is currently working in the United States, the Federal Reserve can print money to finance large trade deficits. This allows American to buy goods that are imported 'without really paying' for them. Ever since it stopped using the gold standard in 1971, the United States' trade deficits have achieved never-before-seen heights. Also, starting in 1995, other countries have taken the fiat dollars that they received as payments for exports and invested them in United States Treasury Bonds (debt). At this point, 50% of the United States national debt is financed by foreign creditors.

A gold standard would also help in restricting the government's ability to increase the national debt. When the government needs to raise money, it issues Treasury Bonds. These bonds are purchased by the Federal Reserve with money that is newly printed. These bonds are supposed to count towards the national debt. Since the gold standard was discarded, the national debt of the United States has increased to $6.8 trillion dollars. It was $406 billion in 1971. This increase has occurred in conjunction with the increase in the money supply. A gold standard would slow or hinder the acquisition of debt by the government. Since the money printed has to have an actual gold backing, printing money wouldn't only require a printing press and paper. It would require actual funds to purchase the gold first. This would mean that debt would not be created as easily. Proponents of returning to the gold standard argue that the United States would not be in debt today at all if it had stuck with the gold standard to begin with.

There are those who speculate that a return to the gold standard could prevent wars that are unnecessary by restricting the amount that the country spends on military and defense. Since the government can print fiat paper money without any limits, it can fund not just military bases outside the country but also go into foreign countries in military interventions that end up being very expensive. In 2011, the United States' defense spending was around $711 million dollars. A return to the gold standard would not allow such expenditure, since it just wouldn't be possible.

The gold standard would also slow the rise in the prices of gasoline and stabilize the price of oil. Saudi Arabia and other OPEC nations had agreed to trade for oil only in dollars by 1975. Since the gold standard had been discarded and a fiat economy was in place, the Federal Reserve was printing more and more dollars. OPEC's decision resulted in the creation of international demand for fiat dollars. The more the fiat dollars flooded world markets, the more a general inflation in oil prices resulted. In 1971, a barrel of oil cost about $20. In 2012, it cost around $100. The gold standard would have restricted this meteoric rise and allowed the price of oil to remain around $1.00 per gallon.

The gold standard is self-regulatory and therefore, the supply of money is in tune with the demand for it. Gold is limited and has to be mined and purified at a cost that is substantial. Therefore, it is produced when the demand for it is high. When a gold standard is in effect, if you need more currency, you need to mine more gold. This raises the market price of gold, and thus encourages the mining of it. More gold is mined until the level of currency is what it needs to be. At this point, the price of gold stops increasing and instead, levels out. Mining too stops. The whole thing is self-regulated. However, under a fiat system, there is no self-regulation mechanism for the production of money.

History has shown that stronger economic growth occurred under a gold standard. During the time that the United States used a metallic or gold standard (1792-1971), the average rate of growth of the economy every year was around 3.9%. Once the gold standard was discarded and the fiat money standard was adopted, economic growth has been at an average of 2.8% every year. This means that had the gold standard remained the economy of the United States would have been larger by $8 trillion dollars today.

The government would not be able to overprint money in order to bail out financial corporations if the gold standard were still in effect. The Federal Reserve has printed huge amounts of new money in the past to bail out institutions such as AIG (the bailout was to the tune of $180 billion dollars). Between April 2008 and August 2009 the yearly money supply growth rate went from 1.5% to 14.3%. The Federal Reserve's balance sheets showed an increase in the yearly growth rate from 2.6% to 152.8% between December 2008 and December 2009. The biggest risk the country faces from such a large expansion of the money supply is substantial inflation in the future.

While the gold standard was in effect, levels of unemployment were lower compared to what they are in the current fiat standard. While the United States was on a gold bullion standard between 1933 and 1971, the unemployment rate was around 5%. Since 1971, the unemployment rates have been at an average of 6%. Income levels, too, rose faster and more during the era of the gold standard. Between 1950 and 1968, there was a 2.7% rise per year in the real median income for males. Since 1971, this increase has been only 0.2% per year. It has been estimated that if the gold standard had continued and if the income levels had continued to grow at the rate that they were growing at in the decades prior to 1971, the average median family income would be higher by about 50%.

As a result of these arguments many prominent personalities such as politicians, businessmen and economists have spoken out for a return to the gold standard. Even institutes such as the Lehrman institute and the American Principles Project are strong advocates of a return to the gold standard. With such overwhelming evidence in favor of the gold standard, therefore, the question arises: why wouldn't anyone want to return to it? What benefits does the fiat money standard provide that the gold standard does not? Let's take a look at some cons of the gold standard that may help answer these questions.

Cons

While it is inarguable that gold has an intrinsic value and globally recognized value, this value is not stable and tends to fluctuate a lot and through a wide arc. Therefore, the gold standard cannot provide the stability that a healthy economy needs. The inflation adjusted price of gold between 1879 and 1933 ranged from $700 in the 1890s to $200 in the 1920s. This was the time of the full gold standard. In 1933, under President Roosevelt, the United States went on a partial gold standard or the gold bullion standard, which lasted till 1971. During this time, the inflation adjusted market rate of gold went from $563 to $201. Even afterwards, once the fiat money standard was in use, the inflation adjusted price of gold has ranged from $2,337 to $1,672 per ounce. Since, the value of the dollar would be determined by the value of gold, in a gold standard economy, it would also mean that these fluctuations could significantly harm the economy. For example, if the value of gold increased or decreased by 15%, the price level of goods overall, across the country, would also end up increasing or decreasing by 15%. No economy could be deemed stable under such circumstances.

Instead of returning to the gold standard, we should focus on making sure that the fiat money standard is well-maintained. There was speculation, in 1981, about returning to the gold standard. In fact, the United States Congress had authorized a study by the United States Gold Commission which would look into a return to the gold standard. This was done to curb the inflation rate, which at the time was sitting at 10.3%. The Commission's conclusions were not in favor of a return to the gold standard. Indeed, by 1982, the rate of inflation was under control, thanks to the policy decisions made by Paul Volker who was the Federal Reserve Chairman at the time. Growth in consumer prices, which had hit a high of 13.5% in 1980, came down to 3.2% in 1983.

Economic contractions and periodic deflations, which are caused by the gold standard, tend to undermine the economy. While a gold standard does encourage economic growth, this growth can outpace the supply of money in the economy. After all, unless more gold is secured to back the money, more money cannot be printed or created. This is when economic contraction and deflation occur. Between the years of 1913 and 1971, deflation occurred during 12 years, the highest of which was -10.5% in 1921, closely followed by -9.0% in 1931 and -9.9% in 1932. However, since the United States has left the gold standard, deflation has occurred only in 2009 and the level at that time was -0.4%.

Another black mark on the gold standard is that a lot of bank failures, financial panics and the prolonged period of the Great Depression were caused by it. Between 1879 and 1933 the United States had financial panics in 1884, 1890, 1893, 1907, 1930, 1931, 1932, and 1933. During the panic of 1933 alone, 4,000 banks suspended operations. Many of these panics were exacerbated by contraction in the money supply caused by the gold standard (more money could not be printed without first acquiring additional gold to back it). Many economists contend that the gold standard played a role in preventing the United States from stabilizing the economy after the stock market crash of 1929, and prolonged the Great Depression. In 1933, when the United States went off the full domestic gold standard, the economy began to recover.

A gold standard would limit the ability of the Federal Reserve to help the economy out of recessions and depressions. Under the current fiat money system the Federal Reserve can use monetary policy to respond to financial crises by lowering interest rates during a recession, raising them during a period of inflation, and injecting money into the economy when necessary. A gold standard would severely hamper it from performing these functions. After the 2008 financial crash, the Fed's TARP (troubled asset relief program) created $700 billion to bail out financial institutions and stabilize the economy. According to Nobel Prize-winning economist Paul Krugman, without the Fed's intervention a "powerful deflationary forc[e]" would have been created. Without the intervention of the Fed it is possible the 2008 crash could have led to another Great Depression.

Returning to a gold standard would limit government's ability to address unemployment. According to Federal Reserve Chairman Ben Bernanke a gold standard "means swearing that no matter how bad unemployment gets you are not going to do anything about it using monetary policy." Under our current fiat money system, the Fed can expand the US money supply by purchasing treasury bonds and the government can use this money to help put the unemployed to work through public spending as the Obama administration did with the $787 billion fiscal stimulus. It is estimated that the 2009 Obama stimulus prevented the loss of about three million jobs. Under a gold standard the stimulus could not have occurred.

Returning to a gold standard could destabilize and crash the already fragile United States economy. The last time the United States moved from a fiat monetary system to a gold standard was in 1879, when the United States returned to a gold standard after the Civil War. The shift caused a massive deflation. Given the current fragility of the United States and global economy, the deflation caused by moving from a fiat money system to a gold standard would severely harm, if not crash, the economy. According to economist Barry Eichengreen, it would be a "recipe for disaster."

A gold standard would increase the environmental and cultural harms created by gold mining. Returning to a gold standard would create increased demand for gold and mining activity would increase. Many gold mines use a process called cyanide leach mining that creates large scale water pollution and massive open-pit scars on the land. Producing one ounce of gold creates 70 tons of mine waste. In addition nearly 50% of global gold mining occurs on indigenous lands, where the communities' land rights are often violated. For example, in Nevada, Barrick Gold is currently engaged in a legal fight to dig out a 2,000 foot open-pit gold mine on Mt. Tenabo, a sacred mountain of the Western Shoshone. Next to the environmental impact, there is of course also the possibility that the gold reserves in the world will eventually be depleted. Though this is not foreseeable in the near future, it is still a possibility. And what would happen if this ever occurred? This could lead to strained relationships between countries, as one countries seeks to gain more gold, but none of the other countries are willing to give any up.

Returning to a gold standard would be a large waste of time, money, and resources. Gold mining and refining is expensive and time consuming. Of course, on the flip side is the fact that an increased need for gold would mean a great number of jobs that are available. According to Barrick Gold (the world's largest producer), an ounce of gold cost $560 to produce in 2012. All the human labor used for mining, refining, and storing gold is time and energy diverted from the real economy. The direct costs associated with a fiat paper money system (paper and printing costs) are much lower (a paper federal reserve note only costs $0.087 to produce). Economist Milton Friedman estimated that for the United States to maintain the gold reserves necessary to back its currency, it would cost 1.5% of the national income.

A gold standard makes the supply of money vulnerable to the ups and downs of gold production. Under a gold standard the supply of money would be dependent on how much gold is produced. Inflation would occur when large gold discoveries were made and deflation would occur during periods of gold scarcity. For example, in 1848, when large gold finds were made in California, the United States suffered a monetary shock as large quantities of gold created inflation. This rise in US prices caused a trade deficit as US exports became over priced in the international marketplace.

A gold backed currency could not expand fast enough to maintain a healthy rate of international trade and economic growth. At current mining rates, the total world gold supply increases about 1.5% to 2% per year, which is not enough to maintain a healthy rate of global economic growth. According to United Bank of Switzerland economist Paul Donovan, the nominal rate of growth in world trade should be around 6% to 6.5%. If an international gold standard were to be re-introduced this growth rate could not be maintained.

Returning to a gold standard could harm national security by restricting the country's ability to finance national defense. In times of war, a quick expansion of currency to finance war buildup is sometimes necessary and a gold standard would prevent this from occurring. In order to help finance the Civil War, President Lincoln authorized the printing of $450 million in fiat currency known as "greenbacks." The United States financed its involvement in WWII in large part by having the Fed print money (which was not convertible to gold by the public since 1933), selling war bonds, and running large deficits. According to Congressional Research Service (CRS) researchers, "the means by which the increase in the money supply came about was through the Federal Reserve's purchase of government bonds. In effect, the Federal Reserve made a loan to the government of newly printed money." By 1946, publicly held debt was 108.6% of GDP.

Returning to a gold standard would be extremely difficult, if not impossible, given the scarcity of gold and the vast amount of money already in circulation in the United States. As of 2012 the US treasury held about 260 million troy ounces of gold reserves. At the market price of gold, about $1,662 an ounce (as of Dec. 27, 2012), that would equal about $434.6 billion in gold. However, the current United States money supply, including cash in circulation and bank deposits, is about $2.6 trillion. In order to peg the dollar to gold, the United States would either have to vastly increase its gold holdings, set the dollar price of gold at $10,000 an ounce, or suffer a massive deflation and contraction in the money supply (or some combination of the three). All the gold that currently exists in the world - about 5.5 billion troy ounces - would be worth about $9.1 trillion dollars at current market prices. Even that is not enough to cover the $16.3 trillion national debt of the United States.

What Were the Benefits of Leaving the Gold Standard?

Although gold retains a certain kind of value recognized all over the world, it does tend to fluctuate quite widely. In fact, between 1879 and 1933, the price of gold jumped from $700 to $200, and when the US was on a partial gold standard, the price of gold fluctuated from $563 to $201. Probably the highest price that gold has ever been was in the 1980s when it peaked at $2,337 per ounce.

Staying on the gold standard meant that the value of the dollar would fluctuate as well, and even a rather small fluctuation of about 10% of the value of money would be enough to destabilize the economy.

Some economists may argue that the ideal way to control inflation is by going back to the gold standard because it limits how much money the government can print and circulate. However, a well-managed fiat money system can actually do the same thing, maybe even better. In 1981, the annual rate of inflation in the US was at 10.3%, and government economists actually mulled over going back to the gold standard to keep the these numbers in check. However, timely monetary decisions made by then Federal Reserve Chair Paul Voker, already stopped the growth of inflation and he continued doing so until it dropped down to just 3.2% by 1983.

Although the gold standard did have a lot of merits, shifting to it from a fiat monetary system would create such a shock in the economy that it might crash. Case in point, the last time the US switched from fiat to the gold standard was back in 1879, right after the Civil War. This sudden shift caused a massive deflation in the country's economy. Now, when the US and the global economy are quite fragile, shifting back to the gold standard would be disastrous to say the least.

It is also virtually impossible to shift back to the gold standard right now, considering the amount of fiat currency already in circulation and the increasing scarcity of gold. As of 2012, the US Federal Reserve reportedly had 260 million troy ounces of gold, which equals to around $434.6 billion. On the other hand, the money in circulation back then amounted to $2.6 trillion.

Going back to the gold standard would mean pegging the cost of gold to around $10,000 an ounce, which is unthinkable. In fact, all the gold in the world today, which amounts to around $9.1 trillion, is not even close to covering the national debt of the United States.

Yes, the gold standard did provide a lot of benefits, like value retention, tighter control over inflation, and the fact that it could allow the government to minimize the national debt, going back to it right now is not feasible.

Chapter 5 - What Money Is, How It Works and What Debt is

Now that we've understood what printing of money is based upon, we're going to turn our attention to the subject of this book – money. Most of us think of money as the paper and coins we exchange for goods and services. However, it is so much more than that. In this chapter, we will look at what money actually is, what backs it and what the difference between national debt and consumer debt is.

What is Money?

We can trace the roots of the word "money" back to the Latin word "moneta." The word itself can mean "unique," but the strongest connection with money is that Juno Moneta was a Roman goddess who was responsible for protecting funds and wealth. Her temple in Rome was the place where the currency of the time was manufactured.

In the broadest sense, money is primarily a medium of exchange or means of exchange. It is a way for a person to trade what he has for what he wants. Ideal money has three critical characteristics: it acts as a medium of exchange; it is an economic good; and it is a means of economic calculation. This does not always have to be in the form of coins or paper bills. In theory, any item could become "money" if it meets the above criteria. However, for our purposes, we will mainly be speaking about the type of money you use today - coins, and banknotes.

Economic Calculation

Money is an expression of exchange value (the exchange values placed on goods by traders in the marketplace). It was extremely inefficient to express the exchange value of goods in units of sacks of grain, shoes, or candlesticks. Out of necessity the market gravitated toward the use of the exchange value of fixed weights of gold and silver. As an example, the original U.S. Silver Dollar was modeled after the Spanish Dollar which had a specific weight of silver (371 4/16th grains of pure silver or 416 grains of standard silver). A simple method of economic calculation consisting of weights and measures greatly improves trade and fosters economic growth.

The second type of money is fiat money, which does away with the need to represent a physical commodity and takes on its worth the same way gold did: by means of people's perception and faith. Fiat money was introduced because gold is a scarce resource and economies growing quickly couldn't always mine enough gold to back their money requirement. For a booming economy, the need for gold to give money value is extremely inefficient, especially when, as we already established, value is really created through people's perception.

Fiat money, then, becomes the token of people's apprehension of worth - the basis for why money is created. An economy that is growing is apparently doing a good job of producing other things that are valuable to itself and other economies. Generally, the stronger the economy, the stronger its money will be perceived (and sought after) and vice versa. But, remember, this perception, although abstract, must somehow be backed by how well the economy can produce concrete things and services that people want.

That is why simply printing new money will not create wealth for a country. Money is created by a kind of a perpetual interaction between concrete things, our intangible desire for them, and our abstract faith in what has value: money is valuable because we want it, but we want it only because it can get us a desired product or service. All printing money accomplishes is inflation, so that money has to regain strength and value every time this occurs.

In order to fully understand money and how it helps create and determine the economy, let's take a look at several different basic economic concepts that are important to understand. These definitions will help you be able to get a better feel for the economy, which can be of great help in building your own wealth and portfolio.

Supply and Demand

Every market runs on the idea of a supply and demand, and in a way, so does currency. When does the Fed decide whether more money needs to be printed? And how? The idea of supply and demand can certainly be applied here, as well. The idea of supply and demand also explains why you can buy last year's TV model for a significant amount less than this year's model.

If we take this example, we know that the TV you are buying is just as brand new as it was the year before. But why is it so much cheaper now? The reason is, because the newer model has the higher demand. A high demand means that people will be willing to pay a higher price for it, because they really want that particular item. In the case of the TV and other technology, our society has very much engrained in us the idea that you are better off if you always have the newest and best technology out there. As soon as an old TV gets outdated, the demand for it drops drastically, and with it the price does as well.

Inflation and Deflation

The idea of inflation and deflation is a very important one to understand if you want to know exactly what makes the economy tick. We talk of inflation when the cost of goods or services goes up for an extended period of time. Take, for example, a loaf of bread. In 1930, a loaf of bread cost an average of 9 cents. In 1950, the cost was already up to 12 cents. The price of a loaf of bread then continued to rise - 22 cents in 1960, 50 cents in 1980, 70 cents in 1990, $2.79 in 2008, and $1.98 in 2013. As you can see, from 2008 until 2013 the price actually dropped, meaning that the economy took a break from long-time inflation.

There are many different theories as to the cause of inflation, and most experts admit that one single cause is rarely at fault for it. A Keynesian economist, for example, will tell you that changes in money supply have nothing to do with inflation. Rather, he believes that inflation is the result of external pressure. Monetarists, on the other hand, believe that the growth and shrinking of the money supply is the key reason for inflation, and that external pressure has not nearly as much to do with it.

Deflation is basically the opposite of inflation. It occurs when the cost of goods or services goes down over an extended period of time. Deflation can be dangerous for an economy, especially if it enters a deflation spiral. This type of deflation is caused because the decrease in price causes production of goods to slow down as well, which again causes prices to decrease. In a way this could also be described as a vicious circle. Many economists believe that the Great Depression was a deflation spiral.

The causes of deflation are also highly debated. One idea is that deflation can be caused by a shift in supply and demand. This can be due to the overproduction of an item accompanied by a drop in demand, or vice versa. Other possible causes include debt or credit deflation and a significant money supply drop for individuals.

Scarcity

Scarcity is the idea that every commodity that can be found on earth has a limit. For example, it is only possible for a certain amount of corn to be grown every year. Some of it may go into ethanol production, some might go into cattle feed, and yet other corn will find its way to your table. Having a solid idea of the scarcity of corn helps a business determine how much of one thing should be produced compared with another. Of course, some commodities are more scarce than others. Gold, while scarce, is definitely not the scarcest or most valuable commodity on earth. Take Iranian Beluga Caviar, for instance. An extremely scarce and hard to get commodity, it can be worth more than $1000 per ounce. And then there is also the exorbitant price of antimatter - a mere $100 trillion per gram. Scarcity certainly has a lot to do with price.

Cost and Benefit

Cost and benefit is a weighing of the expenses and positive aspects of a certain purchase. In essence, it is the idea of a cost benefit analysis. Chances are you are subconsciously doing this all the time.

For example, perhaps you are standing in the cereal aisle at the grocery store. You look at the dozens of boxes of cereal, but you just can't make up your mind. Then you start considering a bunch of different things. First, you look at the price tag. One little trick is that most price tags in stores will not only give you an item price, but will also give you a price per weight unit. This helps a lot, as there are boxes of all sizes in the cereal aisle, so simply just looking at the price won't give you a proper analysis. Then you can also weigh in the benefits. Say one type of cereal has raisins in it, but you know that your family absolutely hates raisins. It may be the cheapest box of cereal on the shelf, but the benefits do not outweigh the cost, so you decide to go a with a different box of cereal instead, even though the cost is a little higher. This is, of course, a very simple example, but the same principle can be applied to everything from buying a car to investing in the stock market.

Paradox of Value

Paradox of value is a simple idea, really. All it means is assigning a high value to something that you do not need. Take engagement rings, for example. They are generally made of gold or silver with a setting of one or more diamonds. A good ring will cost well over $1,000. At the same time, the actual usefulness of a diamond ring is not very great. On the other hand, a gallon of milk has intrinsic value as it helps nourish us. And yet, the cost of a gallon of milk is nowhere near the cost of an engagement ring. This idea is the paradox of value

Money Supply

The money supply of a country is comprised of not only the sum of all the bills and coins in circulation, but also of the sum of all the deposits in the country. This includes everything in any checking or savings account in the country. The Federal Reserve tracks and reports the money supply of the country. The all-time high in the United States was in 2014 at $4.1 trillion, which was all the way up from $48.4 billion in 1961. Some interesting statistics to know are the amount of gold the reserve holds, vs. how much paper currency is available vs. how much money is held in deposit accounts, which are $250 billion, $1.2 trillion, and $2.5 trillion, respectively. In the following we will break down what the exact components of the money supply are and explain them a little more in depth.

Liquidity

Liquidity is how easy it is to sell an asset quickly without having to reduce its value too much. Money, of course, is the most extreme form of liquid asset, but even then, your $1 bill from today is not necessarily worth the exact same tomorrow. Despite this, it is fairly easy to sell your $1 without experiencing too much of a loss. On the other hand, think about the liquidity of a house in an oversaturated market. It is often the case that a home will not sell for the original amount that it was posted at. It can also take years to sell a home. Both of these factors make a home an extremely unliquid asset.

Opportunity Cost

Opportunity cost is an interesting aspect of economics. It describes a loss that you make when you make a choice between two different opportunities. The opportunity that you choose is gained, but the opportunity that you did not choose is lost. For example, you could be in a position where you need to choose between purchasing a car or a pick-up. You cannot have both, as your budget only allows for one. If you choose the car, the pick-up could be described as your opportunity cost. The interesting part about opportunity cost is that it does not always need to be expressed in money. It could also be in the form of time lost or foregone pleasure.

Assets

In very basic terms an asset is an economic resource. Anything that can be owned, whether it is tangible or intangible, can be an asset. The complete assets of a company, for example, include everything from its product inventory, to the office furniture, to the amount of money that is still owed them by other companies or individuals. These different types of assets are classified as current assets, liquid assets, and absolute liquid assets. Your net worth or the net worth of a company generally consists of the sum of all the owned assets.

How is it Measured?

Sure, money is the $10 bill you lent to your friend the other day and don't expect back anytime soon. But exactly how much money is out there and what forms does it take? Economists and investors ask this question everyday to see whether there is inflation or deflation. To make money more discernible for measurement purposes, they have separated it into three categories:

- **M1** – This category of money includes all physical denominations of coins and currency, demand deposits, which are checking accounts and NOW accounts, and travelers' checks. This category of money is the narrowest of the three and can be better visualized as the money used to make payments.

- **M2** – With broader criteria, this category adds all the money found in M1 to all time-related deposits, savings deposits, and non-institutional money-market funds. This category represents money that can be readily transferred into cash.

- **M3** – The broadest class of money, M3 combines all money found in the M2 definition and adds to it all large time deposits, institutional money-market funds, short-term repurchase agreements, along with other larger liquid assets.

By adding these three categories together, we arrive at a country's money supply, or total amount of money within an economy.

How Money is Created

Now that we've discussed why and how money, a representation of perceived value, is created in the economy, we need to touch on how the central bank (the Federal Reserve in the U.S.) can manipulate the money supply.

Among other things, a central bank has the ability to influence the level of a country's money supply. Let's look at a simplified example of how this is done. If it wants to increase the amount of money in circulation, the central bank can, of course, simply print it, but as we learned, the physical bills are only a small part of the money supply.

Another way for the central bank to increase the money supply is to buy government fixed-income securities in the market. When the central bank buys these government securities, it puts money in the hands of the public. How does a central bank such as the Federal Reserve pay for this? As strange as it sounds, they simply create the money out of thin air and transfer it to those people selling the securities! To shrink the money supply, the central bank does the opposite and sells government securities. The money with which the buyer pays the central bank is essentially taken out of circulation. Keep in mind that the example is generalized to keep things simple.

Today there are roughly 1.2 trillion U.S. Dollars in circulation. The U.S. Treasury Department is in charge of printing new money when needed. In 2016 the Treasury Department printed almost 25 million bills per day. When new money is printed, it is sent to the Federal Reserve, from where it is distributed to depository institutions. This means that only banks that take deposits can receive new money directly from the Fed. Mortgage lending banks, for example, cannot.

Of course, you need to remember that not all printed money adds to the total in circulation, as money is also constantly being removed from circulation as it gets worn out. In 2010 alone 2.6 billion $1.00 bills were incinerated. When banks, for example, come across mutilated bills that are torn, have graphiti, or are simply worn out, they send these bills to The Bureau of Engraving and Printing, where it is incinerated. In return, the bank is issued a check. The average lifespan of paper bills is a mere 5 years, so this gives you an idea of how often it needs to be recycled.

Money as Debt

Most of the time, any money that is created comes into existence as debt. Either the U.S. government goes into more debt when it gets more dollars from the Federal Reserve or individual Americans go into more debt when they take out loans from individual banks.

First, let's examine what happens when the U.S. government gets more money from the Federal Reserve. Under the current system, the U.S. government cannot just fire up the printing presses and print a bunch of dollars if it decides that more money needs to be produced. Rather, if the U.S. government needs more money it asks the Federal Reserve for it. So who is the Federal Reserve? The Federal Reserve is actually a central bank that has been given authority by the U.S. Congress to issues our currency, set our interest rates and essentially run our economy. However, the bank is neither privately owned nor owned by the public. It is also not a for-profit corporation. It is run by a board called the Board of Governors, which is in fact a government agency, and yet it is a government agency that is not accountable to the government. The board operates independently and has been given authority by the government to make independent decisions without consulting any branches in government. All U.S. government debt is created through the Federal Reserve System.

It is interesting to note here that the Federal Reserve itself cannot actually be in debt. When it prints money, it does not have to pay for it. In a sense it is commissioned to print money, and the entity commissioning it (the federal government), is the entity that takes on the debt. This is one of the reasons why people in the past and today have called for an audit of the fed. To date the Federal Reserve has never been audited, and it would be interesting to see what they actually have on the books.

When the government wants more money, the U.S. government swaps U.S. Treasury bonds for "Federal Reserve notes", thus creating more government debt. Usually the money isn't even printed up – most of the time it is just electronically credited to the government. The Federal Reserve then sells these U.S. Treasury bonds to investors, other nations (such as China) or sometimes they "sell" them back to themselves.

The Federal Reserve has been called into question by many for actions related to the buying and selling of debt that are defined as quantitative easing. Quantitative easing is a situation in which a central bank, in this case the Fed, buys debt, whether in the form of mortgage securities, Treasury bonds, or other types of debt. Of course, the federal reserve itself can print the money to buy this debt, which in essence simply erases the debts that the Federal Reserve has bought.

Opinions differ on quantitative easing. Some say it is necessary in order to control the amount of inflation or deflation that a currency is going through. Others will say that it is actually a way of manipulating the economy and staying in control. The Federal Reserve has never been audited, and even though it is not a government entity, it is appointed and strongly favored by the government. There are many conspiracies involving the conspiring of the government with the Federal Reserve in order to maintain control of the economy and of the country's wealth. In essence, when the Federal Reserve buys government debt, it funds the government, while at the same time paying off the debt with money it has created. The problem is that the Federal Reserve does not actually add anything of value to the economy, and can be viewed as no more than a tool to manipulate the currency.

Many other countries have similar systems in place. What makes the United States unique, is that its constitution has an amendment that requires the government to pay its debt. In other words, it is not allowed to default or declare bankruptcy. This makes the ability of the Federal Reserve to participate in quantitative easing necessary to follow the law. This is also what makes other countries desire to lend money to the United States government, because it is viewed as a safe debt. They are basically guaranteed by the U.S. constitution that they will get their money back. The danger, however, is that too much money could be printed, which would collapse the entire system.

Recently, the Federal Reserve has used quantitative easing three times in order to control the recessions from 2008 through 2014. During this time the amount of Treasury notes held by the Fed jumped from a mere $700 billion to a whopping $2.054 trillion. This means that amount of debt held by the Fed nearly tripled during this time, which was an unprecedented action up until this point. Supporters of a return to the gold standard strongly disagree with the actions of the Fed, which is part of the reason they want to have their money backed by gold once again. Many feel that the Fed has created an economy that is a house of cards, and could collapse at any moment.

Difference between National Debt and Consumer Debt

Government debt is not like private debt. Government debt need never be paid off. It can be rolled-over. As bonds become due, they are replaced with new bonds. Households can't always do that. Governments cannot be "foreclosed" or "repossessed". Households and their goods can be. Households and private firms can go bankrupt and default. Sovereign governments only default when they choose to do so. Historically the only known instance of a sovereign, floating currency issuing government defaulting was Japan in WWII, but that was deliberate. U.S. and British banks held much of the debt and they were at war. In fact, government debt is necessary to the functioning of a modern financial system. It provides a safe, interest-bearing financial asset.

The key difference is what when a government spends more it doesn't necessarily put it into more debt. In a deep recession, higher government spending induces other people to spend, lifting everyone's income because without the government stimulus no one wants to spend. Remember that when you spend, it's someone's income. Therefore, by spending more the government can, in principle, increase the economy's income and tax revenue and reduce its debt. This mechanism is not available to individuals (they can "borrow to invest", but that's quite different).

Other differences that have been suggested - seigniorage or immortality - have analogies with personal debt. Printing money is a little like losing your job (you're a riskier borrower). Inflation eats away at personal and government debt alike. Immortality of government is not true either since most bonds have finite maturity (at most 30 years, though bonds with perpetual coupons are not without precedent).

Government debts are generally in their own (fiat) currency. So they can always repay them. Your consequences of spending beyond your (income) means are bankruptcy. The government doesn't have that danger; its possible consequences of overspending are high inflation and/or higher rates in future borrowing, but not bankruptcy. Inflation that becomes out of control can lead to devaluing of the currency and eventual economic collapse. So even though bankruptcy is not an option, there is still a risk to government debt with far-reaching consequences.

Using Debt as a Means of Income

Debt is often regarded as a four letter word in our society, and with good reason. Debt is a risk, and in order to incur this risk there has to be a reward great enough to make it worthwhile. This is why using debt only to obtain assets that generate income is a sure way to alleviate debt risk.

Two of the most common forms of debt in modern society are car loans and mortgages. However, neither of these are a means of income in and of themselves. Cars are an especially risky debt, as the value of a car depreciates quickly, and there are not many ways to obtain income through a car. Rental companies would be the exception, or if you drive for a living. A mortgage, on the other hand, has the higher chance of being able to generate income for you, especially if the mortgage you are taking out is on a rental property.

However, even in the two scenarios above, if you are able to make some money off the debt, neither of these options show profit until the debt has almost been repaid. Investments, however, are a different story. Penny stock trading, for example has the opportunity for a very fast return on your investment. The problem here is that in addition to your risk of debt, you are also risking playing the market. As the old saying goes, with high risk comes high reward, but not everyone will be a winner all the time. You need to find an investment that you are comfortable with, and that you know you can get a big enough return on to make your debt worthwhile.

Finally, in order to get a complete picture of today's economy, we need to talk about the stock market. Following we will take a quick look at the history of the stock market and the different types of stocks and investments that are available to you.

Emergence of Stock Trading

When compared with the history of the world, stock trading appears to be fairly new, but it has been around longer than you think. The first major emergence came through the age of colonization and the creation of various trading companies. This was the first chance for people to buy stock in a company. Around this time, the Amsterdam Stock Exchange was the first exchange of the world. It was founded in 1602 by the Dutch East India Company. The London Stock Exchange came quite a while later, in 1773, and it wasn't until 1792 that the New York Stock Exchange was founded.

Until the digital age, all trading was conducted in person on site at the stock exchanges. However, technology had different things in mind. The Nasdaq became the first stock exchange without a physical location. It is an entirely digital platform and allows for much easier trading. Another option that technology enabled was trading internationally. Any modern country with internet access will allow you to trade online. While this has opened more doors to trading than ever, it also requires more and more research and special care on the part of the investors.

Trading Stock

Trading stock means that you are buying and/or selling a share in a company. In order to help create funding, companies that go public will allow individuals or corporations to purchase ownership in the company. The number of shares is determined by the company, but the worth of the shares is determined by the total worth that the company is deemed at, including all its assets, financial and otherwise. That net worth is then divided by the number of shares, giving you the price for one share. Certain types of stock will also pay out dividends on a regular basis.

Trading Commodities

You can still trade commodities today, just like thousands of years ago. However, it is very unlikely that you will show up at a farmer's doorstep and take 100 head of cattle off his hands directly. Just like shares, commodities like these can also be traded on the stock market. It is interesting to note that in the stock market world, metals, including precious metals, are traded as commodities and not currencies. Buying and selling gold or silver is not regarded as currency trading. The nice thing about commodities is that they can diversify your portfolio of investments, which is a statistically wise way of creating wealth. As the saying goes, you never want to have all your eggs in one basket.

Trading Currencies

Currency trading has become quite popular in recent years. For obvious reasons it has a lot to do with money and the value of currency, so we will spend a little more time explaining this type of trading.

Currency trading does not take place at a stock exchange. Rather, there is an entire market dedicated specifically to this type of trading. It is called the Foreign Exchange Market, or Forex for short. However, currency trading was around a long time before the creation of the Forex market.

In antiquity, money changing was already a necessary and respectable trade. Originally, the government had little to do with the private individuals who would exchange your money for a small fee. Currency trading was also mainly done out of necessity, and not for building personal wealth. For example, if you wanted to go to another country you needed to find a money changer so you could get some of the currency of that money. Today, of course, we still trade money for this reason. If you've ever vacationed outside of the country, chances are that you had to exchange your currency for another at some point along the way.

Later, in the middle ages, the Medici family became a powerhouse in currency trading. They had multiple banks set up in multiple countries, and made the trade of currency a large business instead of just one individual's trade. In the 17th and 18th century the hub of currency trading shifted to Amsterdam. This makes sense, as this was the location of the first stock exchange market.

In the 19th century Alex. Brown & Sons, the first investment bank in the United States, became the world leader in currency trading. Of course, the bank also offered other investment options. It began to grow at a time when the modern exchange system was being born. Specifically, many people consider 1880 to be the birth year of modern exchange, as this was the year that the gold standard was started. It is interesting to note that the beginning of the gold standard is closely related to the American Civil War. Due to the factions and unrest, individual states were printing their own money, and there were quite a few different currencies floating around in the United States. In an effort to unify the country more following the civil war, the gold standard was started in order to assist the country with creating a unified currency.

Following the World Wars, Japan became a hub for foreign exchange due to some clever legislation. Gradually, however, the market opened up more and more, as an increasing number of countries dropped their regulations regarding currency trading, making the Forex Market the most liquid market in the world. The Foreign Exchange Market is also the most diverse market in its customer base. Governments, large corporations, small businesses, banks, and individuals all are able to participate in the market. However, over two thirds of all currency trading in the world is done by a mere 10 companies: Citi, JP Morgan, UBS, Deutsche Bank, Bank of America, Barclays, Goldman Sachs, HSBC, XTX Markets, and Morgan Stanley. Most of the names on the list will probably not surprise you.

The idea of currency trading is fairly simple. You trade money in your currency for a currency that you think is going to go up in value. You can then trade it back to the original currency, and your investment will have grown at the same rate as the currency you bought did. The danger here is that it is profitable for you when your own currency is debased. As already mentioned, governments are allowed to trade in currency, as well, meaning that a government can be motivated to debase its currency.

Another reason why a government would want to debase its currency is because it will cause other countries to buy more products, because they have become cheaper. This leads to higher export rates, which is good for the economy. However, if you debase your currency too much you can run the risk of inflation, which can lead to a market crash. One tool for devaluing a currency is the use of quantitative easing, as we have already talked about with regard to the Fed. Recently, it appears that quantitative easing has become more popular among banks around the world. Just last year the European Central Bank performed some quantitative easing that had the result of a debased currency.

As this seems to be a recent trend, more and more economists have become worried about a possible impending currency war and crisis. Countries may find themselves in a race with each other to see who can devalue their currency the most in order to make their exports seem the most appealing. I don't have to tell you that the results of this kind of currency war could be a total collapse of the world economy. However, as long as the governments of the world use these financial tools carefully and in moderation, the problem should never arise.

Hopefully you now have a better idea of how money can work for you and for your government now, in modern day. Next, we will take a look at what the future may hold for money.

Chapter 6 – The Emergence of Bitcoin and Other Cryptocurrencies

Now that you have learned about how money evolved from trading cattle to the coins and banknotes that you are using today, it is time to learn where it is expected to head in the near future. One of the iterations of money that many people believe will be the "next big thing" is cryptocurrency, most notably Bitcoin.

What is Cryptocurrency?

At its most basic, cryptocurrencies are digital forms of money. You can collect, or mine these currencies using computers, called miners. These computers will try to figure out long bits of code, called hashes, from a huge chunk of code called a block. One hash is equivalent to one coin.

One of the issues that many people have about bitcoins and cryptocurrency in general is how the system would prevent counterfeiting. They believe that it is quite easy to create multiple copies of digital items, so what's preventing people from copying bitcoins. However, the creator/s of bitcoin (no one knows who actually invented Bitcoin, but he, she, or they are known by the name of Satoshi Nakamoto) created a way for people to convert all the effort of their miners into digital tokens, which have been proven time and again to be impossible to duplicate.

There are also only a limited amount of tokens available, which effectively makes bitcoins and other cryptocurrencies the digital equivalent of gold. If you own a bitcoin then it either means that you mined it yourself, or someone else did and he/she gave it to you. At the rate at which bitcoins are being mined, it is estimated that the total and final number of bitcoins, which is 21 million, will have been completely mined by the year 2140. Another selling point about cryptocurrency is that it is decentralized, this means that no one group has the authority to make more of it, and it also means that it won't be taken down and made worthless. It also makes this currency and international one that can be used anywhere in the world where bitcoin is accepted.

Besides Bitcoin, there are many other types of cryptocurrencies, and the only things that make them different are the way they operate, but at their very core, they are all legitimate currencies. Since cryptocurrencies have become so varied, there are many different websites that are dedicated to tracking their value, just like you would find on the stock market. You could say that trading in bitcoin is a type of currency trading. As such, it is starting to be accepted as a means of trade on the Foreign Exchange Market, though many traders are still leary about it.

How do You Mine Bitcoins?

How do you actually get bitcoins? You go online, connect to a certain network, and let your computer break mathematical codes. Depending on the complexity of the math problem, you will then receive a corresponding number of bitcoins as a reward. The difficulty of the algorithms increases over time, often depending on the speed and frequency at which they are being solved.

Once, bitcoin miners used their computer's CPU for mining bitcoins, but later on, they discovered that gaming graphics cards were much faster and more efficient at bitcoin mining. However, graphics cards use a lot of electricity, and they produce a lot more heat, so they need proper cooling systems. As you can see, cryptocurrencies are not for the technologically impaired.

Since bitcoin has been around since 2009, it means there are a lot more miners now, and the math problems are a whole lot more difficult to solve. If you try to mine on your own right now, the expenses you will incur will offset the amount of bitcoins you manage to gather. To get around this problem, you can do what most other miners do nowadays, and that is to join a mining pool. Mining pools are collections of bitcoin miners who pool their resources so they can mine bitcoins more efficiently. When you join a mining pool, you stand to mine even more bitcoins than you could possibly have on your own.

Different Kinds of Cryptocurrencies

Bitcoin (BTC)

This is the very first cryptocurrency to hit the mainstream. Bitcoin first went public in 2009 after having first been released to a special mailing list in 2008, and it is still one of the strongest operating cryptocurrencies available. You create bitcoins by using your computer to verify and record payments into a public ledger. Your activities will then get rewards of transaction fees and newly minted bitcoins. You can then exchange your bitcoins for other currencies, products, and services in the real world.

Litecoin (LTC)

Released in 2011, Litecoin is the first cryptocurrency to use the Scrypt hash algorithm. Charles Lee, a former Google employee, released the source code for Litecoin on GitHub on October 7, 2011. Litecoin is essentially the same as bitcoin, but it uses a different hashing algorithm and it also has a slightly improved GUI. Currently, the value of one Litecoin is just a little over $4.

Namecoin (NMC)

Namecoin came from the first "fork" of the bitcoin code, and just like bitcoin, namecoin uses the same algorithm for mining. However, what makes namecoin different from bitcoin is that it has the ability to store data in its own blockchain transaction database. Currently, one NMC is worth about a quarter.

Peercoin (PPC)

Peercoin creators took inspiration from bitcoin; it actually shares a bulk of its source code with its predecessor. However, peercoin uses both proof-of-work and proof-of-stake systems. Being the fourth largest minable cryptocurrency, peercoin now has a market cap of $30 million, but unlike BTC, LTC, and NMC, peercoin does not have a hard limit on the number of coins it can produce.

Dogecoin (DOGE)

Dogecoin came about from an attempt by programmer Billy Markus and Jackson Palmer (member of the marketing team of Adobe in Australia) to create a cryptocurrency that is "fun." You can clearly see their whimsy just by the fact that they used a popular internet meme as the logo and namesake of their currency. Markus said their aim was to make cryptocurrencies more accessible and they also aimed to distance it from the shady dealings that bitcoin is reportedly involved in, like being the main currency used in the Silk Road online marketplace. Dogecoin, however, is one of the lesser cryptocurrencies and is only worth a fraction of a cent.

Potcoin (POT)

This is yet another specialized cryptocurrency that aims to become the standard form of payment for purchasing legalized cannabis, hence the name.

Titcoin (TIT)

Titcoin is the very first cryptocurrency to be nominated for a major adult industry award. Just like Potcoin, Titcoin is also meant for paying for products and services in the adult entertainment industry. This was primarily created to provide anonymity for people who do not want to have any incriminating purchase histories appearing in their credit card records.

Fun Facts about Bitcoin

You can buy a lot of cool stuff using bitcoin. Although there are not that many vendors nowadays who accept bitcoins and other cryptocurrencies as payment, there are a couple of really cool services and products that you can purchase using them. For instance, if you were planning to board one of the Virgin Galactic flights once they become available, you will be happy to know that they are now accepting bitcoins as payment. If you're in the market for a new supercar, Lamborghini actually accepts payments made in bitcoin. Here and there you may also find an ATM that lets you withdraw cash against your bitcoin account.

Bitcoins were once more valuable than gold. The value of bitcoin is constantly changing, but recently it has been going up. In November 2011, due to the market crash, the value of a bitcoin was only around $2, but after it recovered, it topped at more than a thousand dollars per bitcoin.

Bitcoin is banned in several countries. The first country to openly ban the use of bitcoin was Thailand, but they soon after relaxed their ruling and only highly limited its use in the country. On the other hand, China, with its larger economic reach, completely banned the use and circulation of bitcoin in the country, and it remained adamant about its decision until now. A few countries still remain where it is illegal, including Iceland, Bolivia, and Ecuador.

There is only a finite amount of bitcoin. The makers of bitcoin set a rule in place that there will only be 21 million bitcoins in circulation, and the production of bitcoin will be halved every four years until it stops. This means that supplies will last until

2140. This limited run is so the value of bitcoin will remain constant.

There's a hard drive in a dump somewhere that contains an enormous amount of bitcoins. In 2013, bitcoin miner, James Howells, accidentally disposed of one of his hard drives that contained close to 7,500 bitcoins, which was then worth $7.5 million. When he realized his major bungle, he scoured the dump where he believed his hard drive was thrown into, but he never found it.

Satoshi Nakamoto, the founder of bitcoin, is supposedly not a real person. There are rumors that state that a group of people was behind the discovery of bitcoin and they just used the name to hide their respective identities. There are also stories floating around the internet that say the companies Samsung, Toshiba, Nakamichi, and Motorola were the ones that created bitcoin, and the name of the founder was a mishmash of the companies' names.

Whether bitcoin and other cryptocurrencies do become the next phase in the evolution of money or not, one thing is sure, they will be hanging around for a long time. Many people are still a bit apprehensive about using bitcoins for transactions, but you could say the same thing about paper currency when they started circulating. People back then might have thought that a piece of paper could be worth a lot of money.

Of course, there are also those who are of the mindset that money will disappear from the earth entirely eventually. However, most economists will say that this is bogus. While in a Utopian world it is theoretically possible that money is no longer required as everyone lives together in harmony, it is quite a different story when looking at it practically. Whether you like it or not, money is most likely here to stay, and there isn't much you can do about it.

Chapter 7 – Fun Facts about Money

Now that you have learned almost everything you could about the history and evolution of money, you should give yourself a break and indulge in some interesting trivia.

Back in November 2008, the turmoil in Zimbabwe caused an extreme case of hyperinflation. If you thought 10% inflation was high, in Zimbabwe the inflation rate topped at 6.5 sextillion percent; this meant that their money held very little to no value. To give you some perspective, a loaf of bread back then cost more than $300 million (Zimbabwean).

More Monopoly money is printed every year than real money all over the world. Most people do not know that government mints can only print a limited number of bank notes every year. In contrast, hundreds of thousands of Monopoly game sets are being made every year.

Paper money in the US is not really made of paper. What most people don't know is that US dollars are a mix of 75% linen and 25% cotton; this makes the bills a whole lot tougher and harder to counterfeit.

In the Canadian $2 bill, the flag on top of the Parliament building is that of the United States.

In the island of Yap in Micronesia, the native people used Rai stones as currency up until the early 20th century. What made these stones special is that they are massive; some of them actually measure more than 12 feet in diameter.

After World War II, the German Deutschmark suffered from such high inflation rates that people started using them as wallpaper since they held such little value. In fact, it was more cost effective for Germans back then to burn their money for fuel for heating up their homes than to buy firewood.

The first ATMs were radioactive. The earlier models of ATMs needed to use vouchers printed using radioactive ink so the machines can read them.

In 2010, the US government incinerated almost $2.6 billion in $1 bills. Central banks regularly do this so that they can print new money without causing inflation.

According to a study done by the University of Massachusetts, almost 90% of dollar bills in circulation nowadays contain trace amounts of cocaine.

Queen Elizabeth II holds the record for appearing in the most number of currencies. As of present, the Queen Mother has had her face printed on currencies from 33 different countries. She first appeared on money when she was still 9-years old.

The gambling industry actually generates more income than the music, sports, and movie industries combined.

It actually costs more to create one penny. If you do the math, it costs the US government 2.5 cents to mint a one-cent coin. This is why many countries all over the world have completely eliminated their one-cent pieces from circulation; countries like Canada, Brazil, and Australia do not have one-cent coins anymore.

If Bill Gates, the founder of Microsoft, were to spend $1 million a day, he would need 218 just to get through his entire fortune, and that's assuming that he stopped earning money on the day he started his spending spree.

The "metallic" smell you get on coins actually came from the skin oils of the numerous people who have touched it decomposing on the surface.

If you are ever unfortunate enough to get some ripped up dollar bills, you can send it to the Federal Reserve and they will send you a crisp new bill; as long as you still have at least 51% of the original bill that is.

The largest known counterfeiter of US currency is actually North Korea.

There are more than 50 different slang terms for money in the English language. A few of them include benjamins, bucks, clams, dough, greenbacks, lucre, smackers, and wampum.

Ever wonder where you dollar bill has been before it reached you? There's a website for that, and it's called www.wheresgeorge.com. If you receive a dollar bill with the website printed on it, this means that you can go online and log it into the website, as well as see where it was in the past. This program is an official bill tracking program that is supposed to help study the flow of money.

Conclusion

Thank you for reading this book about the history and evolution of money. By now, you probably have a deeper and more meaningful understanding of currency. Before you even picked this book up, you might not even have given any thought about the coins and bills you have in your pockets, but now that you know all of the things that they had to go through to get where they are now, you now appreciate them even more.

I hope that your journey towards understanding money won't end here. There is so much more to learn, and with all the information available to you on the internet, you could spend hours and hours researching money and financial ideas. Finance and the economy are an incredibly complex subject, and understanding it is not always easy, so thank you for taking the journey together with me in the book. If you are really interested in the subject, there are often great classes offered at community college, as well.

I also hope that using money has become a little more meaningful to you. When you pay cash the next time you go to the gas station, and that dollar bill passes through your hands, you can remember the rich history that goes along with it, and the complex system that makes it work - as long as people continue to have faith in it. And whatever you do, don't lose faith. Your entire economy is counting on you!

Be thankful that we no longer have to trade livestock and produce anymore, and that you no longer have to save your money in piggy banks in your home. By now, you are probably excited about where the next evolution of money will be; will it go the digital route like Bitcoins and other cryptocurrencies, or will it branch out into other, yet undiscovered mediums? Regardless, I hope that you enjoyed the journey through this book, and that it has helped to enrich your understanding of money.

LEAN STONE
BOOK CLUB

Join the LEAN STONE BOOK CLUB today!

To stay up to date on new releases, promotions and all the good stuff, then join our book club email list today!

When you join, you will receive a **_free VIDEO course_** on speed reading.

Go to the link below to join the crowd right now

www.leanstonebookclub.com/join

Made in the USA
Las Vegas, NV
08 February 2022